5852
Albert Geronimo

Lee Templeton
AR B.L.: 4.3
Points: 3.0

Albert Geronimo

Albert Geronimo

Lee Templeton

EAKIN

Library of Congress Cataloging-in-Publication Data

Templeton, Lee, 1920–
    Albert Geronimo.

    Summary: When a friend releases a pet alligator on Lee's farm, its continued growth creates both fun and problems.
    [1. Alligators — Fiction.   2. Farm life — Fiction]   I. Title.
PZ7.T256A1   1986   [Fic]   86-16587
ISBN 0-89015-561-5

A dedication to my brother, Pat

This story, though partly fiction, is based on some of the experiences I had with my brother, Pat, years ago. His full name was Pat Neff Templeton. He graduated from high school in 1939 and then attended North Texas State University and The University of Texas at Austin.

In 1941, Pat enlisted in the Royal Canadian Air Force at the age of eighteen (the U.S. Air Force did not accept pilots under age twenty). Pat was piloting a British bomber in England when his plane crashed on September 7, 1942. He and the four crewmen who were with him are buried at Bicester Military Cemetery in Bicester, England. His RCAF number was R97834.

Pat had planned to be a lawyer. He was fearless, courageous, and stubborn — and he was an animal lover. If he had become a lawyer, the courts would have had to get accustomed to his entering the courtroom with a mountain lion or grizzly bear and have it sit next to him where he could ask it to help him pick a jury. No one ever communicated with wild animals more intimately than he did.

Contents

Chapter 1

The Start of It All

Lynn Courtney was a friend until he bought a pet baby alligator on a trip to Florida. He was even my friend when he got home with the alligator. In fact, he was my friend plum up 'till he told me he got tired of taking care of his baby alligator and turned it loose in a creek we have on our farm.

I thought about it a long time before I told Daddy. I must have thought about it half a day.

Lynn told me at noon on the day school started, the first of September. Said he couldn't take care of the alligator now that school started. He didn't want to kill it, so he dropped it in the water where the creek runs off our place onto the state highway. Lots of people throw away things at our bridge, where there's water and a bridge and big trees to hide what they're doing. We're used to finding dogs and cats and old mattresses thrown out at the bridge.

Trouble was, we always found a home for every dog and cat that was thrown away. People got used to getting rid of unwanted animals by tossing them out at our place.

Me and my brother Pat would doctor them if they were sick and feed them 'till they were fat and healthy. Then we'd find them all a home — sometimes at our house.

But our place was no place to leave a live alligator. Mostly on account of we have dogs, cats, chickens, hogs, and milk cows. Especially milk cows. We make our living milking cows. We milk twenty-five cows every day, and we milk them twice a day.

I had heard that alligators eat dogs, cats, and chickens. But I didn't know what *all* they ate until I told Daddy that Lynn Courtney had turned a pet alligator loose in our creek.

"What?" Daddy shouted, turning white and dropping his milk bucket.

"Lynn Courtney turned his pet alligator loose in our creek."

"He couldn't have!" Daddy stared at me in disbelief.

I laid my book satchel on the living room table and took my lunch pail in the kitchen. They serve lunch at school, but I prefer my mama's cooking. Those women at school don't know how to make doughnuts, or homemade biscuits, or homemade fried sausage. And nobody ever could bake an apple pie like Mama.

Anyway, when I got back to the living room, Daddy was still standing there by the door with his arms outspread over his dropped milk bucket. He hadn't moved an inch since I told him about the alligator.

"No," Daddy said, shaking his head at me hopefully. "Not even Lynn Courtney would do that."

"He did."

"How do you know? Were you there?"

"No, but he had a pet baby alligator that he got when they took their Florida vacation, an' he told me in school today he couldn't take care of it no longer and that he turned it loose where the creek runs under the highway."

Daddy just stood there, sort of in shock. It was as if he had been hit real hard but didn't believe it.

2

I decided to try to say something good. "That bridge is where everybody turns their pets loose."

That must have helped some because Daddy dropped his arms. "But an alligator is no pet. Especially not on our place. We don't only have pets and calves an alligator would eat, we also have little children. An alligator would eat a little boy or a little girl as quick as it would a cat or a dog or a pig.

"No, an alligator is no pet," he continued. "They are reptiles. They'll eat anything they can catch. And what's worse, we have a swamp. That makes our farm a perfect place for an alligator. We have to find that alligator and kill it. The quicker the better."

"If we find it, do we have to kill it?" That was my brother Pat speaking. He didn't like to kill anything. He liked to doctor birds with broken wings. He walked out of the way to keep from stepping on a red ant. Of course, he was just barely old enough to go to school, only in the third grade.

Dad turned toward Pat. "Yes, we have to kill it. Even if it's a baby, we have to kill it. If we don't kill it, some day it will be big and then it might kill us."

"I'd rather just catch it," Pat grumbled.

Daddy and I stared at Pat. Pat was a most unusual little brother.

If you lost something real bad, like a bottle of poison, you know who'd find it? Not me or Mama or Daddy or my sister Tina. Nope, no matter how hard we looked, we wouldn't find it. But Pat would. And when he did find it, he'd stick it in his mouth between his teeth and come running with a big smile as wide as his fat face. And he'd never hand it to you with his hand. Not my brother Pat. He'd stick out his head and make you take it out of his mouth. And he'd probably laugh and not turn loose of it the first time you reached for it.

We didn't get a chance to look for the alligator until Saturday. Instead of fishing in the swamp or roping fence posts, we spent the whole morning looking for a twelve-inch baby alligator. We didn't let Pat go; maybe that's why we didn't find it. It was just me and Daddy and Lynn Courtney and his dad.

We started at the bridge, at the very spot where Lynn said he turned the alligator loose. We took sticks and beat every bush, every mossy spot, every clump of grass. I'll bet we covered every inch of the creek, all the way from the bridge to the swamp. There was no way to check the swamp. It was half a mile long and as wide as a city block, and it was covered with moss and mud and willows and cattails. You couldn't find a full-grown alligator in that swamp, and a baby alligator was plum out of the question. Unless maybe you sent Pat in there. And that was out of the question, too, even though he was a finder. Especially if you lost something dangerous. If black widow spiders were to become extinct, my brother Pat would find one.

Somehow I knew that if that alligator were ever found, it would be by some quiet, slow-moving person — like my little brother Pat.

He found him all right, but not until the next summer. He told us about it on July 2. Pat was ten by then and already dreading the thought of next year's school. The fourth grade.

We were at the dinner table and Mama was talking about what she was going to fix for dinner for July the 4th. Then she mentioned eggs.

"I would fix an angel food cake if the hot weather hadn't caused our hens to quit laying eggs." Mama still had that bright look in her eyes that said she was somehow going to find enough eggs for an angel food cake. If she baked an angel food cake, we always got two cakes. She used the whites of the eggs to make the angel food cake, and then she'd take the yellows of the eggs to make a pound cake.

Pat broke in with his solemn voice. "Tina's taking

4

too many eggs to Armbruster's store buying candy and ribbons and black garters."

Tina dropped her fork. "I give you some of the candy." She glared at Pat and stuck out her tongue. "You ole tattle-tale!"

Mama shook her head. "Something's happening to our eggs."

Tina glared at Pat. "Pat takes more eggs to the swamp than I take to the store."

"To the swamp!" Daddy suddenly looked up from his plate. Pat wasn't supposed to go near the swamp. But he always did.

Even Daddy, busy as he was, knew that Pat spent hours at the edge of the swamp, watching frogs, turtles, and red-winged blackbirds. Sometimes he'd give himself away, telling how many ducks he saw or how many wild turkeys. And the black mud on his shoes told Mama where he had been. When he went down there with me to bring in the cows to be milked, he would stay with the cows 'til they headed for the barn. Then he'd turn back for the swamp, and maybe not come to the barn 'til milking was done or it was dark, whichever came first.

Pat was looking at Tina instead of Daddy. Then after he scolded her with his glance, he looked at Daddy.

"You been goin' to the swamp?" Daddy wiped his hand on a white linen napkin.

Pat nodded his head.

"You been taking eggs down there?"

Pat glanced at Tina, then back at Daddy. Then he nodded his head.

"What in the world you been taking eggs to the swamp for?" Daddy asked.

"A friend of mine," Pat answered, cutting his eyes from Daddy to me.

"Oh, you got a friend down there," Daddy laughed. "Must be an awful expensive friend. How many eggs does he eat a day?"

"One a day." Pat glanced down guiltily. "But sometimes he don't get one for a whole week. Sometimes two weeks."

"What kind of a pet you got?" Daddy asked.

"Just Albert. I'm the only friend he's got."

"Oh, Albert." Daddy smiled. "I guess we have enough eggs to spare one a week for your friend Albert."

Pat glanced at Tina again.

"This Albert," Daddy had his tongue stuck out the corner of his mouth as he leaned over, slicing thick slices off a big baked ham. "Is Albert a possum or a coon?"

Pat shook his head, leaving crumbs of corn bread in the corners of each side of his mouth. "Nope," Pat smiled that guilty little grin of his, "Albert ain't no possum and he ain't no coon."

"Well," Daddy sat back in his seat, staring at Pat, "what is Albert?"

"He's just a friend of mine. Likes to have me scratch his back."

"And he likes eggs, too!" Daddy laughed.

Everybody went back to eating; that is, everybody except Mama. She picked up a dishcloth, but she never looked at it. She just looked at Pat with worried eyes. She had the dishcloth between her hands and raised it almost to her chin, in a sort of prayerful position. She leaned across the table toward Pat.

"This Albert," Mama asked, "is he the alligator we couldn't find last September?"

Pat looked up and suffered for an instant. Pat never lied. He was independent as an eagle and silent as a horned toad. He didn't say anything. He just nodded his head.

Every knife, fork, and spoon at the table suddenly came still and then was dropped, banging noisily in the silence.

"What!" Daddy exploded, spitting bits of corn bread. He grabbed a napkin and rose from the table. "You mean . . ." He stalked toward Pat. "You mean you been feedin' an alligator?"

Pat had his head down, looking at his plate. He nodded.

"But why?" Daddy demanded.

Pat's head rose slowly, and big tears streamed down his cheeks. "I been feedin' Albert. He's my friend. He don't have no other friend. I been feedin' him eggs and bread and pieces of meat. We're real good friends."

"An alligator?" Daddy's face looked as if it would explode.

"Well," Pat pushed back from the table and rose about belt-high to Daddy. "You got a horse you feed all the time and never ride. Mama's got a canary bird that don't do nothing but sing. Tina's got a cat, and Lee . . ." he was now pointing at me, ". . . Lee's got a dog, and me, I ain't got nothing, nothing but Albert."

Mama got up from the table and came over with a napkin and wiped a tear off Pat's cheek. "But Son," she raised Pat's chin a tiny bit until his big blue eyes met hers, "you can't keep an alligator. They're dangerous."

"Not Albert. That's why I have to feed him. He ain't big enough to eat anything, and besides, he's in a pen and can't get out to scrounge anything. That's why I'm feeding him; he'd starve to death without me feeding him."

"You've got him in a pen?" Daddy's eyes brightened.

"You know that old fish box near the slough on the east side of the swamp?" Pat sat back at the table and began forking slices of ham on his plate. He raised his head, gulping a big forkful, licking his lips. He chewed and shifted food in his mouth and then swallowed. Then he smiled proudly. "I fixed it up. I put chicken wire over the top and made a sliding door out of a piece of plywood. It made a nice safe home for Albert."

"You mean you got that alligator in a box?" Daddy interrupted. "How did you ever get him in?"

"Just picked him up," Pat grinned. "He's got sharp teeth, sharp as needles. But if you clamp your hand over his mouth, he can't use 'em, can't even open his mouth," Pat laughed.

"You put the alligator in a box? By yourself?" Mama asked.

"Aw shucks, that was nothing." Pat grinned, wiping his hands on a napkin. "I put him in the box two or three times a day."

"You mean he escapes?" Daddy rose from the table, looking down at Pat.

"No, Dad, he don't escape. I take him out for walks."

"You what!" Now Mama stood up.

"Aw, Mama, if you love something, you can't leave it in a pen all the time. You have to take it out for walks, to play and roll in the mud and prowl in the cattails."

"You didn't . . ." Daddy shook his head, "you didn't let it get back into the cattails."

"Just about every day," Pat laughed. "Sometimes I had a little trouble finding him, but now when I want Albert, all I have to do is whistle and he comes scrambling. I always feed him or offer him food right after I whistle."

"You go whistle him up right now." Dad pointed his finger at the door. "We're going to . . ."

Dad's voice trailed off as he glanced around the table, finding everybody gazing at Pat with admiring smiles.

"But he's asleep now," Pat objected from his chair.

"How do you know he's asleep?" Daddy's voice sank.

"We had a real long walk and he was plum tired when I put him in his pen. He's plum tuckered out. He always sleeps after a long walk."

"Henry," Mama came toward Daddy, fingering the edges of her apron the way she always did when asking for something, "don't you think we could let Pat keep him as a pet for a little while? After all, he found him, he raised him as a pet, and kept him out of harm's way. I know how he feels. He has mothered that baby alligator just like I mothered him."

"Oh . . . Well . . ." Dad glanced around him, knowing he was outnumbered. "We raise everything else, why not raise an alligator?"

"Thanks, Daddy." Pat went over and shook hands
with Dad. "You'll like Albert. We'll let you take walks
with us. Maybe I won't have to hide him no more. I might
start me a zoo and start charging admission so I'll have
enough money to feed him."

"Zoo!" Dad sunk in his chair.

"Yeah," Pat grinned. "I think a zoo would be lotsa
fun, don't you?"

Daddy never said anything. He just stared at the
floor.

Chapter 2

Albert Gets a Full Name

It was late in the evening of the next day when I walked up on Pat sitting on the sunny eastern side of the spring-fed swamp. His two-foot alligator was asleep in his lap. The alligator opened one and watched me until I sat down. Then he shut his eye and seemed to go back to sleep.

"Why'd ya give that stupid smilin' alligator a name like Albert?" I asked as I chewed on a blade of grass. "Why Albert?"

Pat shrugged.

"He does smile at you all the time, doesn't he?"

"Yeah, he pulls back his lips and sort of grins and shows his teeth."

"Why'd ya give a smilin' alligator a name like Albert?"

"Well, I thought about Prince Albert, but a baby alligator can't look much like a prince." Pat shook his head sadly.

"You can say that again," I agreed. "Why'd you name him Albert?"

"Well, Albert sounds like somebody that's real quiet and minds his own business. And besides, he's so sad-faced." Pat shook his head. "He thinks I'm the only friend he's got in the whole world."

"Is Albert the only name you're gonna give him? Ain't you gonna give him no last name?" I asked.

Pat looked up. "I hadn't thought about no last name."

"Well most likely he ain't gonna live long enough to need no last name, anyway."

"He is, too!" Pat's eyes flashed fire. "He's gonna live as long as me or you or anybody. An' he's gonna have a last name, too." Pat reached down and stroked the scaly back of his alligator. Then he looked up at me. "How about Geronimo? He's got a sad grin and a wrinkled face like an Indian chief."

"Aw, Geronimo's too long. You can't even spell a name that long."

"I can, too." Pat got up, setting his alligator on the grass gently. He walked to a sandbar at the edge of the creek. In the sand he wrote, "J-e-r-o-n-i-m-o."

"You don't spell Geronimo with a J. You spell it with a G."

"He's my alligator, ain't he?" Pat asked.

I nodded.

"Well, if he's my alligator, I can name him any name I want to, can't I?"

I nodded.

" 'Sides, I can't write a G very good, but I can write a perfect J."

I nodded.

"Well, you don't hear him complainin', do you?" Pat argued.

I shook my head and laughed. "He's just wrinkle-eyed and dry-skinned enough to look just like that old Indian chief." I looked at Pat and then at his alligator. "If he's gonna look like Geronimo, ya oughta at least spell his name like the real Geronimo, with a G."

Pat looked at me. His jaws were set and his lips were tight and unhappy. Then he looked at his alligator. A little smile creased his cheeks. He leaned over the sandbar and erased the J with his hand. Slowly, with the tip of his tongue sticking out the side of his mouth, he replaced the J with a G. Pat sighed and turned away from me. "Can't even name my own alligator."

Chapter 3

An Unexpected Guest

As the summer weeks passed, Pat and Albert Geronimo were always together in the cool evenings. The little long-mouthed alligator followed Pat on his long walks around the swamp every evening about milking time. Then one morning Albert Geronimo followed Pat to the house.

Our old dog, Big Mack, was the first to complain. First he raised his ears. Then he rose to his feet, not believing what he saw. Big Mack stood there with his tail sticking straight out as Albert waddled toward the back porch, following Pat. But as Albert got closer to the house, Big Mack barked once and took off around the side of the house with the hackles along his back raised. He looked back at Albert and ran, his tongue hanging out of his mouth and his tail tucked between his legs. He stopped at the front porch and looked back at Albert one more time. Then he jumped onto the front porch swing and tried to climb the chain that fastened the swing to the roof of the porch.

Just then Albert seemed to want to hurry Big Mack

13

up and make him jump and yip. All Albert had to do was open his ten-inch mouth and show his bright rows of pearly-white teeth.

Tina's cat, Pricilla, had a fit climbing the willow tree near the back porch, and Tina screamed. But me, I just grinned and announced, "Daddy, I see Albert's come visitin'."

"Albert?" Daddy looked up from reading his newspaper. "Who's Albert?" He started to turn the pages of his paper. Suddenly, he jumped to his feet and threw the paper aside. "Albert!"

Daddy looked out the front door and saw Big Mack climbing all over himself trying to reach the highest point on our porch swing.

Daddy ran out the back door, and there was Pat sitting on a log near the wood-chopping block, with the alligator's horny head resting against his feet. Pat was leaning over, patting Albert on the head. The two looked like brotherly companions.

"We're gonna have to get rid of that thing." Daddy pointed at Albert. "He's got Big Mack howlin' and climbin' the chains on the front porch swing, and look at Pricilla up there in the tree." Daddy pointed at the cat. Pricilla was on the tallest limb of our willow tree, swaying in the breeze and probably wondering if cats really have nine lives.

Pat didn't pay much attention to anybody. His calmness spoke louder than words. He rubbed Albert down his spiny back, and Albert had his eyes shut and his head snuggled up against Pat's feet. He was almost snoring, he was so content.

Tina came forward and leaned over, looking at Albert. "Is he dead?" she asked.

Pat shook his head. "Naw, he ain't dead. He's just sleepin'." He looked up at Tina. "Alligators do a lot of sleepin'. Ever'thing that's ugly has to do an awful lot of sleepin' tryin' to get pretty."

Tina wiggled her nose and tossed her head. "I don't sleep any more'n you do."

Daddy let a little smile turn up the corners of his mouth. "That alligator sure sent Big Mack running for cover and Pricilla up the tree, didn't he?" He looked at Pat.

"Good thing Mama wasn't here. She would've climbed that willow tree higher than Pricilla." I looked up at the cat on her perch in the tree.

"Yeah, and faster," Daddy laughed.

"Good thing she's gone to the grocery store."

Tina grabbed a handful of dirt and threw it at Albert.

Albert opened one eye, then opened the other eye. He raised his head slowly and shook it as the sand rolled off. Then he opened his mouth and flashed his shiny white teeth at Tina. His mouth looked like somebody opening the door to the storm cellar.

Albert growled, and Tina ran to hide behind Daddy.

"We can't keep an alligator here, Son." Daddy spoke to Pat as Albert lowered his jaw and rubbed his chin on Pat's shoes.

"Albert didn't throw no sand at Tina. She threw the sand. All Albert did was tell her to be a good girl."

"Well, he can't stay here, Pat. Your mother would take one look at him and she'd faint."

"He eats mostly frogs and snakes and turtles and cattail roots. He won't hurt nobody 'er nothin'," Pat said. "I think it oughta be like you say the law is; I think he oughta be innocent until he's found guilty. He oughta be given a chance."

Daddy rubbed his chin. "But what if he was sitting on the front porch and your mother had a club meeting with all those dressed-up women, and one of those women walked up on the front porch and saw Albert?"

We all laughed.

"What if he met Mrs. Gatewood and her Pekinese pup?" Daddy laughed. "When he opened that wide mouth, she'd jump plum out of her girdle."

"That'd be fun, wouldn't it?" I volunteered.

"Yeah, but Mama would faint, and she never would have club again," Daddy pointed out.

Tina's little brown eyes brightened at the prospect. "Yeah, that'd be something to think about."

Daddy raised his foot and offered Albert a bite on his heavy boot.

Albert raised his head an inch or two, sniffed at Daddy's boot, and then laid his head back down on Pat's shoes.

Pat looked up at Daddy. "Albert's mighty particular. He don't eat but ever' two weeks."

"Is that why I still got a boot?" Daddy laughed.

"Albert won't eat nobody." Pat picked Albert up and hugged him around the neck.

Mama never fainted more'n three or four times. She came in and found Albert sleepin' on Pat's belly near the warmth of the kitchen stove. Woke 'em both up. Pat got scared, but Albert didn't. Albert didn't even get mad when Pat spilled him on the floor.

"Get that reptile out of my kitchen!" Mama screamed.

Pat got up and motioned for Albert to follow him out the kitchen door onto the back porch. Pat turned to Mama. "Ma, it's nearly September and it's gettin' colder. School's fixin' to start. Albert gets cold, and he likes to sleep in warm places, like beside the kitchen stove."

"Get him out of this house!" Mama raised her finger and pointed to the back door. "That alligator is no pet. He's just waiting to get big enough; then he'll eat you."

"No, Ma, he won't eat me. He likes me, an' besides, he don't eat but ever' two weeks," Pat protested.

"And he might decide to have *you* for breakfast one of those cold mornings."

Pat reached down and picked Albert up and carried him out the back door. He set him down on the ground between the door and the willow tree. Pat leaned down and patted Albert. "You wouldn't eat Pat, would you?"

Albert didn't move or make a sound. But Pat noticed that his eyes were following Pricilla as she raced up the trunk of the willow tree, glancing back as she climbed, hoping alligators couldn't climb trees.

Chapter 4

Albert Meets His Match

Queen Victoria was no ordinary red-haired spotted sow. She had long floppy ears, a white curly tail, and was as long as a boxcar. She was not only big, she did everything in a big way. When she had pigs, she had at least a dozen, and she protected them like each one was a prince or a princess.

Queen Victoria had every kind of hog blood that a hog can have. She had Duroc red hair, Yorkshire white ears, the brown spots of a Spotted Poland, and she even had a dark Hampshire stripe across her chest.

Queen Victoria wasn't just a good mother; she was a bossy sow. If the United States Marines started a fight with Queen Victoria, they'd lose. She'd not only whup 'em, she'd have 'em saluting and feedin' her shelled corn before the day was half over.

Yeah, I'd say Queen Victoria's one hog I wouldn't want to cross swords with. Me and Daddy already knew it. And Albert learned pretty quick.

We had a fine hog house for Queen Victoria to use when she got ready to have pigs, but she never would use it. She would take off down to the creek. She'd cross the swamp and get in the willow and cottonwood trees and make her a bed. She'd bite off weeds and grass and willow twigs and make a circular bed. Then she'd lie down and have her pigs. And believe you me, nobody, and I mean nobody, would come close to her. She was like Grandma when she was out of snuff. Not even a grasshopper was allowed to land near her bed. Even the red ants had to turn around and go the other way.

Queen Victoria would lie there on her bed for four or five days. She would nuzzle her pigs and teach them to suckle. Nothing or nobody was allowed to come close. She even raised her hackles at a mockingbird if it flew over and dropped a shadow on her bed.

I was watching her once when she ate a watersnake that came close to her and her pigs. It happened so quick that neither me nor the snake knew what happened. She raised her head and twitched her ears, then grunted and jumped to her feet. She ran about five steps and stomped her front feet, jumping up and down. Then she reached down and came up with the writhing snake clamped in her jaws. She chawed a couple of times and swallowed a couple of times, and that was the end of that snake.

Queen Victoria met Albert right after she had fourteen pigs. She had been down in the breaks below the swamp and was on the way to the barn with her pigs trailing along behind her.

Queen Victoria met Albert about halfway between the barn and the swamp. She weighed 500 pounds, and it'd be a mighty wet day if Albert weighed twenty-five.

Albert opened his storm-door mouth and growled and hissed.

Queen Victoria's red hackles raised on her back. She looked behind her at her fourteen pigs, and then she looked at Albert. She tossed her head and pawed the ground with one front hoof. Then she made a running stampede at Albert.

Albert heard the freight train coming. He opened his

mouth as wide as it would open and began hissing and growling. Then he got real smart and started backing up.

Queen Victoria stopped and stood her ground, pawing gently at the grass with her front foot, trying to figure out what Albert was.

Albert continued to back up, hissing and growling and snapping his jaws. He and Queen Victoria had met, and Queen Victoria had come out the winner.

It was a good thing Albert didn't look like something good to eat, or else he would have been the pigs' milk. Queen Victoria didn't walk out of anybody's way, not even Daddy's. Only two things interested her, and that was hog feed and her pigs. If Albert had made a move toward her or her pigs, Queen Victoria would have bit him in two and ate him up before he knew he was caught.

When Albert got out of sight of Queen Victoria, he turned his head, sniffing of her fourteen pigs. His head was sadly dragging the ground as he crawled away like a whipped dog.

Chapter 5

Readin', Writin', and Reptiles

From what I hear, Pat nearly ruined Mrs. Phillips and the entire fourth grade class the first morning he went to school.

It was about ten o'clock and time for recess. Mrs. Phillips was reading a story. She heard something scratching on the classroom door.

"Come in," Mrs. Phillips called out.

Pat gritted his teeth, shut his eyes, and gulped. He knew Albert's scratch anywhere, even outside the door of the fourth grade classroom.

When the door didn't open, Mrs. Phillips rolled her chair away from her desk and got up. She walked toward the door with a smile. "Whose dog followed who to school this morning?"

Pat managed to raise one hand before Mrs. Phillips got to the door. She was such a nice, sweet, kindly person.

"That ain't no dog, Mrs. Phillips." Pat rose from his desk just as Mrs. Phillips opened the door.

Mrs. Phillips smiled sweetly as she opened the door. She looked out the door and saw no dog. Then she low-

21

ered her eyes and screamed loud enough to peal the bell in the tower of the Lone Pilgrim Primitive Baptist Church. She threw her ruler in the air and turned, white-faced, to her students. She said, "It's an . . ." Then she fainted and fell to the floor.

Even after Mrs. Phillips fainted, Albert was still outside the door, and the class was still sitting at their desks.

Then Albert crawled through the door and raised his long snout over Mrs. Phillips. He smiled at Pat and crawled over Mrs. Phillips as he headed straight for his master's desk.

Sadie Donnell, with her red hair, freckled face, and big glasses, sat in the front row next to the door. When she saw Albert, her glasses flew out in front of her, her hair rose straight up, and she brought one hand to her mouth in a gasp. Then she rose straight up in the air, kicking her feet, climbing air stairsteps as she screamed like a thousand roaring freight trains.

With Mrs. Phillips on the floor, Albert could see Pat inside the classroom. He began clambering across the school room, and when he did . . .

Sadie Donnell's scream was nothing.

Big fat Henry Holmes tore his desk from the floor as he stood up. His eyes were as big and white as light bulbs. He backed into the rear wall, bouncing the first time he hit. But the second time, he bulldozed right through without ever taking his eyes off Albert's happy crawl.

Tall and skinny Jesse Culpepper's dark skin turned white. He took one look at Albert's toothy grin and dove through the window. By then everybody was going through windows, doors, and walls.

Mr. Longnecker, the principal, heard the tornado in the fourth grade room and arrived just in time to get run over in the stampede. His bald head and long skinny neck were all anyone could see before he disappeared — that and his big, disbelieving eyes.

Albert never paid any attention to all the commotion he caused. As far as Albert was concerned, there was only one person in the room. His Pat. He headed straight for Pat, paying no attention to the broken desks, busted windows, and scattered chairs. He grinned his usual big toothy grin when Pat picked him up and cuddled him next to his chest. Pat started carrying him out of the shattered classroom.

Mrs. Phillips raised up long enough to faint again when she saw Pat carrying smiling Albert out of the classroom.

Mr. Longnecker was on his hands and knees when Pat walked by carrying Albert. His eyes were bigger than white coffee cups. It was easy to see he still didn't believe what he saw. He turned his head, following Pat and Albert.

"I think maybe I'd better take Albert home," Pat spoke as he walked by the shoe-splattered face of Mr. Longnecker.

"Albert?" Mr. Longnecker whispered as he crawled around the classroom on his hands and knees.

Chapter 6

Goin' Shoppin'

"What'cha makin'?" I asked Pat.

"Alligator carrier." Pat spoke without looking up. He was making something out of cotton cloth.

I crowded a little closer and looked over Pat's shoulder. "What'd you say you was makin'?"

"I'm makin' a carrier so Albert can go where I go," Pat explained.

"You gonna carry Albert? He's nearly as big as you are!" I protested.

"I'm gonna make a carrier that I can strap on my back so he can ride on my back and look over my shoulder."

"What's the matter with him walkin'? He's got four legs an' you ain't got but two."

"He don't like the hot sidewalks. He don't like hot concrete."

"You're not gonna carry him downtown!"

Pat bit some thread between his teeth and broke it off. He spat out the thread and looked up at me. "Why not?"

I waved my arm, pointing toward the road to town. "An alligator just doesn't go walkin' downtown."

"Why not?"

"Women will scream, merchants will faint, and policemen will have heart attacks."

"Albert ain't swallowed nothin' bigger'n a baseball. Don't see why they'd be afraid of a li'l ole alligator."

I shook my head and smiled. "Well, don't go carryin' him downtown in a pack on your back with his head stickin' over your shoulder."

"Why not?"

"Well, where would you take him?" I asked.

"I thought I'd take him to Armbruster's. You see, Albert, he don't eat but about ever' two weeks, an' he ain't had anything to eat in nearly . . . well, almost ever' bit of two weeks. I thought I'd go in there and get him some meat an' bone scraps or something."

"You're not gonna carry a two-foot alligator on your shoulder that hasn't eaten in two weeks?" I asked.

"Why not?"

"He's liable to bite your head off!"

Pat turned and looked at me with a knowing grin on his face. "Not Albert. He's my friend. He wouldn't bite me. He goes where I go. He even went to school with me."

"Yeah, I heard about that. He ended school for the rest of that day."

"Yeah, they wanted to shoot him. I had to take him home."

"Well, you can't take him in Armbruster's. He'd tear the place up just like he did the school."

"Aw, I've already called Mr. Armbruster."

"You have?" I asked.

"Yeah, Mr. Armbruster said I could bring any animal in there I wanted to as long as it was on a leash."

"Did you mention Albert?" I pointed to the alligator pack that Pat was making.

Pat nodded his head quickly. "Yes, I did. I asked Mr. Armbruster if I could bring my Albert, an' he said as long as I had him on a leash, he would be welcome in Armbruster's."

"But did you tell him that Albert is an alligator?" I asked.

Pat looked at me wistfully and slowly shook his head.

It was Friday after the second week of school that I went with Pat to Armbruster's Store and Meat Market to get some meat and bone scraps for Albert.

Mr. Armbruster is a big, thin-faced, jolly Norwegian who likes to help kids with their pets.

"You say you need some meat and bone scraps for your pet?" Mr. Armbruster tore some white wrapping paper off of a circular wrapping stand. "I didn't know Big Mack needed meat and bone scraps. You've never asked for any before." Mr. Armbruster started pulling bones and hunks of fat out of his sawdust trash barrel.

" 'Tain't for Big Mack," Pat volunteered.

"Oh, for Pricilla then." Mr. Armbruster was trying to find out how much of the meat scraps he needed to put on top of the white paper wrapper.

"No, it's for Albert."

"Oh, Albert. That's right; you mentioned him. You've got a new addition to the family?" Mr. Armbruster stood still and rolled his eyes. He knew Pat, and now he remembered hearing about . . .

"Not very new." Pat looked at me as he spoke.

"Not new?" Mr. Armbruster turned to Pat with wide eyes. "These meat and bone scraps are not going for that terrible, that horrible . . ."

Pat nodded.

"Not for that alligator!" Mr. Armbruster shook his head.

Pat nodded.

"You mean for the alligator that caused Mrs. Phillips to faint and caused the kids to go through the walls of the school?"

"They didn't go through the walls of the school.

There was some screamin' an' some desk-climbin', and Jesse Culpepper and Andy Wallace jumped through the window. But there weren't nothin' to it. I just picked up Albert and carried him home. I think Mrs. Phillips needed smelling salts, but when I got back after taking Albert to the swamp, school was goin' on fine."

"But Pat," Mr. Armbruster left his meat scraps on the wrapping paper and walked toward Pat, "there's a question about feeding an alligator."

"There is?" Pat asked.

"Yes, there's an old African quotation that says, 'Never feed an alligator thinking he will eat only your neighbors.' "

"That's why I want some meat and bone scraps, so he won't eat Pricilla. Our cat's about to have a nervous fit climbin' up and down that willow tree. She's wore a path out."

"Well, I'll give you these meat and bone scraps, but I hope you don't kid yourself that you can feed an alligator to keep it from eating you."

Pat and I looked at each other with misgivings as we carried the package of meat and bone scraps out of the meat market.

The next day, Pat and I took off for Armbruster's with Albert on a leash. At least it was a leash when he started. Albert didn't like being led on the end of a leather bootlace tied over the two front teeth of his bottom jaw.

Albert didn't go very fast. And he didn't go where Pat said for him to go. He went where Albert wanted to go. Fortunately, since Armbruster's had a meat market, Pat didn't have any trouble following Albert into Armbruster's once they got to town.

Down the aisles Albert led the way, frightening ladies with baskets of groceries. He climbed the fruit displays, grabbing an apple here, a peach there. He nosed a cantaloupe onto the floor, held it between his front feet, and gulped it into juicy bits, slinging the yellow seed all over the floor.

"No, Albert, you can't do that." Pat jerked on the leather bootlace leash. Albert paid no more attention to the leash than he would a fly on his back.

Pat looked at me with wild, helpless eyes. I shook my head. Pat reached down and picked Albert up just as he finished the last of the cantaloupe.

"Let's get outa here," I whispered, ducking low to hide behind the aisles of food.

"Gotta see Mr. Armbruster." Pat pushed the scattered cantaloupe seed into the corner of the aisle with one tennis shoe. He looked up at me with wide, suffering eyes. "I gotta pay for an apple, a peach, and a ripe cantaloupe."

"Yeah, and if you don't get Albert outa here, there's no telling what else you'll have to pay for."

Pat stuffed Albert inside his shirt, frowning and blinking his eyes as Albert's tail flipped and flopped. He made his way slowly toward Mr. Armbruster at the white weighing scale at the rear of the store.

Pat reached down with both hands, tugging at the wiggling alligator inside his shirt.

"Mr. Armbruster, will you charge my dad for an apple, a peach, and a cantaloupe?"

"How's that?" Mr. Armbruster stopped carving a side of beef and looked up.

"Can you charge my dad for an apple, a peach, and a cantaloupe?" Pat looked down guiltily.

"Well, I suppose so." Mr. Armbruster smiled and held out his big hand. "If you'll hand 'em to me, I'll weigh 'em."

"Huh?" Pat stepped back, taking a tighter grip on Albert's wiggles.

"I have to weigh fruit; we sell it by the pound," Mr. Armbruster insisted.

Pat looked down at Albert wiggling and clawing around his belly.

Pat shook his head. "It's too late to weigh it now."

"Oh, you've already eaten it?" Mr. Armbruster's eyebrows rose as he eyed me and Pat. "And a cantaloupe, too?"

Pat nodded.

Albert suddenly got still. I could hear him sniffing and snorting. Pat's eyebrows rose. Then Albert began to squirm around a lot. He smelled something.

Mr. Armbruster turned his back just as Albert's head popped out of the front of the neck of Pat's shirt. He had smelled the meat. Now he could see it. He started climbing out of Pat's shirt.

Pat wiggled his hips and pushed Albert back inside his shirt just as Mr. Armbruster finished making out the charge ticket on the fruit. He handed it across the meat counter toward Pat.

Pat looked at the charge ticket and reached around his chest with both hands just as Albert's head was about to pop out. Pat turned to me. "Maybe you'd better sign the charge ticket," he mumbled as he turned and kept his back to Mr. Armbruster.

"Well, I didn't get no apple or peach or cantaloupe," I argued.

"You didn't?" Mr. Armbruster looked at his ticket, then at me, and finally at Pat, who had his back turned to Mr. Armbruster. His shirt was wiggling something awful.

"Hmm . . . I'll sign the ticket." I stepped up to the meat counter. It was obvious Pat couldn't sign nothing. He looked like a girl doing a hula dance — with a snake in her shirt.

Pat and I stumbled out of the meat market, mostly walking backwards. I was in front of Pat, who had both arms filled and wrapped around his shirt. He was trying desperately to keep Albert Geronimo's wiggles inside his shirt. Albert Geronimo was trying desperately to stick his head out and see what happened to the meat.

Chapter 7

Pat Makes a Deal

"Would you sell me your Boy Scout pack?" Pat asked when I got in from school one day. He gets outa school half an hour before I do, and he was waiting for me at the mailbox across the county road from our house.

I shook my head. "No way." I shifted my books as I walked by him, noticing him drop his head like the world had come to its end.

He trotted along behind me. "You didn't pay but $3.98; it can't be worth more'n four dollars." He caught my free hand to slow me down so I could watch him put on his sad face.

" 'Tain't for sale." I skipped up the front porch steps, Pat still trailing along behind me holding my hand that had no books. I jerked my hand loose, shifted my books, and pushed open the front door. I wasn't about to turn around and watch Pat. He was putting on his act.

As the front door slammed, I heard him. His voice was choked like a martyr about to be shot. "You don't ever go to Boy Scout meetings. You ain't even gone on a hike."

I turned and shouted through the front door. "I can't go on Scout hikes. I have to milk the cows," I growled.

Pat ran through the front door before I could turn around. "I'll milk the cows for you!" His blue eyes were big and wide. He was no longer the martyr; he was now the trader. "If you'll give me the Scout pack, I'll milk the cows for you. For a week. For a whole week."

I shook my head. "You ain't good enough. You leave too much milk in the cows; you don't strip 'em."

"Two weeks," Pat bargained.

I stood there staring at Pat's pleading eyes and his begging, outstretched hands. I tried to shake my head again, but his big blue eyes wouldn't let me. If Simon Legree had met Pat when he wanted to trade, Simon Legree would have traded his mustache and his whip for a blade of grass and wondered how he got such a bargain.

When Pat wanted something, he wanted it bad. Terribly bad. He would trade all his tomorrows for just one today.

Anyway, I traded him my Boy Scout pack for two weeks of him taking my place doing the milking with Daddy. Then, when I found out what he was gonna do with my Scout pack, I felt like Simon Legree; I figured I hadn't made a very good trade.

"What'cha gonna do with my Scout pack?" I asked as I set my books on top of the radio, thinking of two weeks without having to milk cows twice a day.

Pat smiled and blinked his blue eyes. "Gonna make a back pack and put Albert in it so I can take him wherever I go."

I stopped in my tracks and turned slowly. "You're what?" I could suddenly see Albert the alligator having to do my two weeks' milking.

Pat was smiling and grinning as he lifted Mother's scissors out of the sewing machine cabinet. "I'm gonna cut a hole in the bottom of the pack for Albert's tail, and I'm gonna strap him on my back and take him everywhere I go."

I shook my head. I kept shaking it, but Pat kept nodding and clipping the blades of Mama's scissors.

Chapter 8

Alligator Transportation

It was late in the afternoon when Pat strapped Albert in my Boy Scout pack and shouldered him on his back. Albert struggled a couple of times 'til he found out he was securely strapped. Then he gave up and just grinned. He seemed to like whatever Pat did. Albert put one front leg on Pat's shoulder and the other on top of his head, and laid his long snout on the back of Pat's head. It was Saturday afternoon and two hours before milking time.

Pat looked like a boy with a alligator's head, except Albert kept looking around all the time. Now and then he'd look behind him. Every once in a while Pat would reach up and pet Albert on top of his head.

They really did look like an alligator walking on his two hind legs, 'specially to half-blind and spectacled Miss Libby.

Miss Libby lived 200 yards down the road toward town, but I heard her scream like she was two feet away.

I looked at Tina, and Tina looked at me. She shut her

eyes and put her fingers in her ears. Mama and Daddy were gone to the store.

I had taken one tennis shoe off to pour the hot sand out of it, but I ran anyway. Miss Libby was screaming louder than the fire whistle when a tornado is approaching.

I could see Pat and Albert walking down the middle of the road. I was afraid Albert might get scared and bite Pat's head off. Miss Libby was staggering back and forth in her front yard. She'd wave her arms, and then she'd touch one hand to her forehead and the other to her chest, like she was fixing to faint.

Pat kept walking on down the road. I noticed he shifted Albert until the alligator's head was on Pat's other shoulder, the shoulder next to Miss Libby's side of the road. Now she could see Pat's head, and it looked like it was almost in Albert's mouth.

Miss Libby went rigid. Her arms stuck straight up in the sky. They trembled and shook, and I heard her gasp, "An alligator's eaten Pat Templeton!" She fainted and fell backward, bouncing like a dropped fence post.

Pat walked backward a step or two, looking back at Miss Libby, who was now still and quiet. Then he shrugged his shoulders and walked on down the road.

When I got to Miss Libby's gate, I looked at her and then I looked at Pat. He was nearly to town, walking down the road with Albert slung over his shoulder in the Boy Scout pack. Pat and the alligator glanced around and smiled at me like two grinning boys eating ripe watermelon. They knew they hadn't done anything wrong.

It looked like Miss Libby needed attention — bad. I didn't open the gate; I just jumped over it. I got to her real quick-like, but then I didn't know what to do. I wanted to pick her up, but if I did, I'd have to run my arms under her, and that just didn't look right. I bent over her this way and I bent over her that way, but there wasn't any way I could pick her up. She was as big as I was.

I finally put one arm under each armpit. With her head bouncing against her chest and her feet dragging, I drug her to her front porch, up on the porch, and through the front door. I laid her on the divan in the living room and started looking for a telephone. I ran into the kitchen and looked in there, and then I looked in the hall and in the bedrooms, and then ran back to the living room. I couldn't find a telephone anywhere. I knew she had one, because she had called Mama lots a times. That's who I was gonna call if I found a telephone.

Well, Miss Libby was on the divan looking like she was either dead or gonna die. I decided I might oughta take off and catch Pat and Albert 'fore somebody else fainted.

I ran out into the front yard and jumped the gate. There wasn't any sign of Albert or Pat. I ran toward town first, and then I turned around and ran back toward our place, and then I ran back toward town again. I had to find Pat. I had decided this carrying an alligator in a Scout pack on Pat's back wasn't worth getting out of two weeks' milking.

I really ran. Then way ahead of me I saw Pat and Albert still going down the middle of the street, toward Pickett's Store. Pat turned to the right and started walking on the sidewalk. He was walking up behind heavy-set Mrs. McNeil. She was wearing a straw hat that had red and white feathers bouncing on the side, feathers that looked like birds. I started running as fast as I could to try to catch Pat and Albert.

Pat waved his hand at Mrs. McNeil as he passed. Of course, she couldn't see Pat's head; it was on the other side of Albert's head. Just then Albert raised his head and climbed a little higher on Pat's shoulder. He reached his snout over and snapped Mrs. McNeil's straw hat right off her head and began munching it.

Mrs. McNeil reached up and grabbed where her hat had been. She turned and looked nose to nose at Albert, who was feasting on her straw hat. Mrs. McNeil threw her hands up and jumped out of her shoes. She gasped and raised her hands up high. Her hands touched some bananas hanging near the wall of Pickett's Store. "Snakes!" she screamed and jumped again, and when she hit the wall, she fainted near the flour barrel.

Albert and Pat turned around and leaned over Mrs. McNeil. Albert raised his head and bit a banana off Mr. Pickett's bunch of bananas and munched it with big, grinning jaws.

I ran up beside them. Pat was looking at Mrs. Mc-Neil's false teeth, which she had evidently lost when she fainted.

He turned and looked at me like he had never seen false teeth before. Mrs. McNeil looked a little odd, layin' there so still with her teeth layin' on her necklace.

I raised Pat and turned him around. We ran across the street toward Scovil's Ice Cream Store. Albert was still chewing Pickett's banana, grinning his long, toothy grin.

Chapter 9

The Swimming Hole

Saturday afternoon I was on the front porch, sitting on the swing with my feet taking up all the swing. Tina was standing in front of me with her arms folded across her chest, waiting for me to move my feet so she could sit on the swing. Pat was swatting flies against the front screen door with Mama's fly swatter.

"Swing me." I smiled a big-brother-to-little-sister smile at Tina.

She shook her head, grinning her little sister smile, watching and waiting for the swing to stop swinging.

When the swing was almost still, Tina nodded her head, wiggling her yellow pigtail, following the almost stilled motion of the swing.

"When you put your feet down, I will sit in the swing." Tina studied me with folded-arm determination.

I stepped out of the swing. "You can have the screechy old swing." I looked over at Pat. "Let's go swimming," I suggested.

Pat had his fly swatter raised, but he turned his head to me. "It's hot 'nuff." He raised his head thoughtfully and dropped the fly swatter on the floor of the porch. "Could I take Albert?"

"Could I go?" Tina hopped out of the swing.

"Naw, you can't go. You're a girl." I pushed Tina out of the way. Then I turned and looked at Pat. "Albert?" I asked, then shook my head. "I don't think I'd wanna swim if he was in the pool."

"I didn't wanna go anyway, if that alligator's goin'." Tina swelled up with her hands on her hips.

"You can't go and Albert can't go." I pushed Tina into the swing and gave it a huge push, making her grab the sides of the swing to hold on.

"Let's go." Pat came up to me with his big fat-faced grin. "I'll race you to the swimming hole."

I shook my head. "It's too hot to run."

The swimming hole was down the creek from our place, across the county road, on the Davenport place. Grapevines hung from huge trees there, furnishing living "swings" that could be swung over the water.

We were walking slow and I never looked behind us. I knew Tina wouldn't follow, but I plum forgot about Albert — and Albert followed Pat almost everywhere he went.

I began whistling at Rusty Davenport before we got to the swimming hole. He came running off the back porch, shading the sun from his freckled face before I whistled my second whistle. I made the motion of diving and swimming with my hands. Rusty nodded. Then I saw him wave his arms.

I stopped. Rusty wasn't waving his arms at us. He was waving at somebody else. Somebody in Sunday go-to-meetin' clothes, leaning against the big cottonwood tree in the Davenports' back yard.

Pat and I both stopped.

"That looks like Harvey." Pat stomped his foot. He turned and looked at me with disappointment.

"Harvey ruins everything." I looked at Pat and then looked at the narrow path to the swimming hole.

"He'll want the water tested 'fore he sticks his big toe in." Pat looked back down the trail, wishing he was back on the front porch swatting flies.

"Has he ever swung out over the water on a grapevine?" I asked.

Pat shook his head. "He'll have to ask his mama to test it first." Pat scowled. "Harvey won't even smoke grapevine bark."

"Oh well, cummon. Maybe he won't get in the way too much." I laughed. "Maybe Harvey won't find a bush clean enough to hang his clothes on. Maybe he'll just watch. If he just watches, he won't get in our way much."

"Harvey will. He always gets in the way." Pat was glum.

We walked on down the trail. Rusty Davenport and Harvey Millhouse ran down the hill from the Davenport place, and Rusty was waving his arms, but not Harvey. Harvey walked very slow, being careful not to step on any cow manure in the Davenport cow pasture.

Pat was half undressed, plum down to his pants and shoes, by the time we got to the swimming hole below the tiny waterfall. "Last one in's a rotten egg!" Pat shouted as he dropped his shirt and straw hat on the grass near the water. He dropped his britches and began untying his shoes, but one of the shoelaces had a hard knot.

Rusty Davenport dove in first.

Pat was trying to pull off his shoe without untying the knot, but it wouldn't come off. I dropped my clothes on a clump of grass by Pat as I ran by him, patting him on the shoulder, shouting "Rotten egg!" I dove and grabbed a thick hanging grapevine and swung out over the water, kicking my feet, enjoying the cool shaded air speeding by my naked body. I grabbed my nose as I turned loose of the swinging grapevine and dropped feet first into the water.

Wow! It felt good! Cold spring-fed water. I splashed over and ducked Rusty's head under the water and swam away grinning 'til he came up. Then I raced him for the shore. I grabbed my hanging grapevine as I climbed out.

Just as Rusty was climbing out, I jumped on the grape-vine and kicked him back into the water.

Pat finally got his shoe untied and dove in just as I turned loose of the grapevine and dropped into the cool water.

After my third swing into the water, I saw Harvey Millhouse leaning against the big oak tree next to the pool. He was fully clothed and he had that "holier-than-thou" look. His nose was raised and his eyes said he thought the water was getting muddy. He looked like he was glad he was clothed. It made me want to get him wet.

When Pat saw me watching Harvey, he came over to me.

I nodded my head toward Harvey Millhouse. "Let's go baptize ole 'High Hat' Harvey."

Pat nodded, and we both swam slowly toward Harvey with mean, mischievous grins on our faces.

Harvey wasn't looking at us. He was just looking at the water, watching it muddy up after each dive. He was still standing between the tree and the water when Pat and I climbed out of the pool.

Then he saw that look in Pat's eyes. He jumped a bit and started to run, but he ran into the tree. Pat grabbed him low and I grabbed him high, and we pulled him to the ground.

"I'm gonna tell my mama," Harvey shouted as Pat got him by his hands and I got him by both feet. We swung him back and forth a couple of times to gather speed and height. Then we let him fly into the deepest part of the water, clothes and all, just as he kicked and shouted, "I'm gonna tell my — "

Before Harvey hit the water, Pat and I saw something swimming in the water, right below Harvey as he was coming down. We stopped and stood still. Then we shut our eyes.

There was Albert Geronimo! In the swimming pool! He was swimming toward Pat, grinning his long-snouted toothy grin.

Harvey came down square on top of Albert Geronimo.

Albert and Harvey saw each other about the same time, except Albert wasn't up in the air, coming down. He could move. All Harvey could do was scream and shut his eyes.

Pat and I looked at each other, then back at the splash where Harvey and Albert got acquainted. Albert came up first. He opened his mouth — about fifteen inches. That was what Harvey saw when he came to the surface.

"Alligator!" Harvey shouted, spitting water at Albert. He was too scared to swim; he just splashed water.

Rusty Davenport hadn't seen Albert. He had been running up the hill, holding on to the swinging grapevine. Down the hill he came, swinging out over the water. He looked down just as he turned loose of the grapevine.

Albert Geronimo was right under him, looking up, with his fifteen-inch mouth wide open.

Rusty had started to reach for his nose, but when he saw Albert under him, with his fifteen inches of bright shiny teeth, Rusty forgot all about his nose and turned in mid-air and tried to grab his grapevine. But it was gone.

Rusty did his best to stay up there in the air. He kicked and reached and grabbed and looked below him. But gravity didn't help Rusty one bit. He came down on top of Albert Geronimo and Harvey Millhouse.

The three disappeared below the water briefly. Rusty was the first one to come up, kicking and splashing.

"Alligator!" He spewed water out of his mouth and churned water with both hands. He sped to shore, dove up on the grassy bank, and pulled his legs out of the water. Looking at his feet, he began counting his toes. "There's an alligator in there!" He shouted as he climbed to his feet and raced away from the swimming hole.

Harvey splashed to the surface, trying to walk on water. Albert came to the surface with Harvey, but

Harvey was between Albert and Pat. So Albert headed for Pat. Harvey was right in his way.

Harvey turned white and fainted. It took me and Pat both to pull him out of the pool.

Harvey ain't never been the same since. He sees alligators every time he sees me or Pat. He don't faint; he just turns white and starts running, looking over his shoulder at us, shouting, "I'm gonna tell Mama . . ."

Chapter 10

Bully Bart

"I'm gonna make me a pair of cowboy boots outa that alligator." Barton Riley mashed a forked stick down on Albert's neck, holding him in place. He reached over and felt of Albert's horny back. Then looked up. "Reckon he's big enough to make a pair of cowboy boots?"

"Ain't nobody gonna make no boots outa my Albert." Pat stalked up to Bart Riley. The top of Pat's head came to the bottom of Bart's shirt pocket.

"Who's gonna stop me?" Bart laughed.

"Me an' Lee, that's who." Pat pointed his forefinger at me.

I shook my head and stepped back, trying to find a place to disappear.

"You an' Lee an' who else?" Bart laughed again, pressing the forked stick harder into Albert's neck, causing Albert's tail to rise and flip in pain.

I had already backed up to the cottonwood tree at the corner of Washington and Lee. It used to be in Bart's yard before they widened the street. I figured I couldn't back up no further, so I hollered, "Now Pat, don't be gettin' me in your fights."

Pat looked at me. He could see I was looking for a good opportunity to get behind that cottonwood tree. Pat bit down on his jaw and tightened his lips. Then he looked up at Bart Riley. He must've got a crick in his neck lookin' up that high, but he looked him square in the face.

Barton Riley was way too big for Pat to fight. He was too big for me an' Pat *both* to fight. Nobody even in the eighth grade could whup Bart Riley. Bart liked to fight; he fought all the time.

Pat put his hands on his hips and spoke very firmly. "You take your stick off of my alligator."

Bart Riley looked down at the alligator penned by the forked stick around his neck. Then he looked at Pat. "Take it off yourself." Bart doubled up one of his fists as he spoke.

Pat raised one foot slowly and deliberately, like he was fixing to take a big step. He shut his eyes and stomped his foot down on top of Bart's foot.

Bart screamed and bent over and grabbed his foot, and when he did, Pat kicked the forked stick off of Albert.

Pat grabbed Albert around his belly and raised him up so that he was staring into Bart's face. Albert opened his mouth almost a yard wide as Pat pushed him at Bart.

Bart ducked as Albert snapped, just barely in time to save his nose. He ducked so hard and so fast that he fell.

Pat stepped over Bart, straddling him. He held Albert above Bart so that Albert's wide-open mouth and bright, shiny teeth were against Bart's nose. As he pushed Albert's snout against Bart's nose, Bart's head lowered until his hair was in the dirt. Then Pat pushed Albert a little further.

"No! No! Don't let him!" Bart flinched and turned his head to the side.

"Hold still." Pat bent over low, rubbing Albert's

snout against Bart's nose. "What'd ya think, Albert? Would he make a good pair of boots for an alligator?"

"No. Huh-uh. No, I wouldn't." Bart Riley's face wrinkled up like he was fixing to cry. "Get this slobberin' alligator off of my nose."

Pat squeezed Albert's belly and the alligator's mouth opened wide. "He don't like the way you slobber, Albert." Pat jerked Albert's body back just as his wide jaws snapped shut a couple of inches from Bart's nose. "Wonder what he'd taste like, Albert? Reckon he'd taste good?"

Bart was shaking his head, rolling it from side to side. His left ear got dirty on one shake and his right ear got dirty on the next shake. "I wouldn't taste good. Really, I wouldn't," Bart pleaded.

Pat pulled Albert back a few inches away from Bart's face and cradled Albert's body in his arms. "We're gonna let you go this time, Bart Riley, but if you ever mention the word 'boots' around me an' Albert again, I'm gonna let him bite your nose off." Pat stomped one foot. "Plum off."

Pat raised one foot slowly and moved away so that he was no longer astraddle Bart. He walked away about as victoriously as Napoleon Bonaparte would have moved after his biggest win in battle.

Pat gave me a very disappointed jerk of his head as he walked by me with his nose up in the air.

Pat and Albert had whupped Bart Riley, nearly made him cry. And they never even hit him once.

When Bart finally rose to a sitting position in the road, the first thing he did was touch his nose. When he got to his feet, he felt of his nose again to make sure it was all there.

Chapter 11

Albert Meets Tarzan

Pat liked to take Albert everywhere he went — even to the picture show.

One Saturday afternoon Mama and Daddy took us to town. Pat and I put Albert in the trunk of our old car.

When we got to town, Pat waited at the car until Mama and Daddy went into Armbruster's Store and Meat Market. Then he stood leaning against the trunk, waiting for Tina to go away. But Tina just stood there.

"Well, ain't you goin' to the show?" Pat asked.

Tina stood beside the car, watching Pat with narrow, suspicious eyes. "I'll go when you and Lee go."

Pat shook his head and looked at me and winked. "I ain't ready to go to the show."

"Are you gonna just stand in the street leaning against the car in the sun?" Tina asked, noticing that Pat was staying close to the trunk.

"If you wanna see *Tarzan*, you better go on," Pat growled.

Tina finally shrugged her shoulders and walked away. She stopped every few steps and looked back.

45

"Go on! Go on!" Pat shouted, waving his hand at Tina for her to hurry up and disappear.

Tina stopped in front of the Ritz Theater. She stood with her hands on her hips for a long time. Finally, she tossed her head, walked up to the booth, and paid her ten cents to get into the show. She stepped back and took a last look at Pat.

Pat was grinning mischievously at me. When he was sure Tina was in the theater and wasn't gonna take another look at him, he spoke. "Have you got a dime for Albert?" Pat grinned.

I shook my head. Then I looked at Pat again. "You're not gonna take Albert into the show!"

Pat nodded. "There's an alligator in that show."

"You're not gonna take Albert in there!"

Pat nodded again. "I want Albert to see what an alligator really looks like. I want him to see how they live."

"He already knows what an alligator looks like," I insisted.

"Albert don't know; he ain't seen no other alligator," Pat argued.

"Yeah, but Tarzan kills that alligator."

"Well, he might not," Pat argued.

Pat glanced around him and then opened the trunk of our car. He picked Albert up and stuck him inside his shirt. Then he looked at me. "You reckon they'll charge a dime for Albert? He ain't ten years old."

"If they can't see him, they can't charge, can they?" I grinned.

We started toward the show with Albert wiggling and twisting inside Pat's shirt. Pat was having to hold Albert with both hands.

When we got to the pay booth, Pat looked at me. "Maybe you'd better pay my way in." He handed me his dime.

We walked in there like there was just two of us.

I heard Albert sniffing when we walked by the popcorn case. Pat grabbed Albert just as his head was about to pop out of Pat's shirt.

Pat turned to me. "Maybe we'd better not buy any popcorn."

"Okay. Maybe we can buy some on the way out."

We ran down to the front row. There were three empty seats there on the front row where we always sat, but they were next to Tina. Pat shook his head.

We took a seat in the third row in the middle of the theater, having to crawl by some grown men and women. It wasn't until after we sat down that the lady next to Pat began to rattle a paper sack and eat popcorn.

Pat shut his eyes and gave me a "yipes" look. He had trouble holding Albert even before the picture show started.

When the curtains rolled back and the show started, Pat unbuttoned the top button of his shirt and Albert's long snout stuck out. Albert looked around and lunged at the lady's sack of popcorn. Pat grabbed him just before his snout snapped out.

He looked down at the floor and then he looked up at me and whispered, "Maybe we're in the wrong place."

"Yeah, I think we're in the wrong place."

"I ain't leavin'; I'm gonna see this show." Pat pushed Albert back into his shirt.

"Somebody's gonna lose their popcorn," I whispered.

Pat got Albert back inside his shirt and held him just fine until the elephant stampede scene. But while Pat was grinning and clinging to the arms of his seat, Albert reached over and snapped the popcorn bag out of the lady's hand. He leaned forward with a big grin on his face as he ate the sack — popcorn and all.

I heard the lady turn to her companion and say, "I do believe that's the ugliest boy sitting next to us that I ever saw in my life." She looked at her empty hand where her popcorn sack had been and whispered to her companion, "And he's rude, too."

Pat and I both got to watching the show and forgot

about Albert, especially when Tarzan howled and beat his chest and swung through the trees on grapevines. Pat looked at me and winked. After all, we swung on grapevines at the swimming hole.

When Tarzan dove into the water and started swimming after an alligator that was about to catch Jane, Pat felt of his shirt. His eyes went wide and he looked at me.

"What's the matter?" I asked.

"Albert's gone."

"No!"

"He crawled out the bottom of my shirt."

We felt of the floor and the seats around us, looking around, waiting to see where lightning would strike.

The scream came from the popcorn booth. An ordinary scream is bad enough in a Saturday afternoon picture show, but this was no ordinary scream. It shook the rafters. Everybody in the theater jumped to their feet. The lights suddenly came on.

Pat and I started wrestling our way out, feeling like a couple of caught pickpockets. When we got to the popcorn booth, there was Albert, tearing open his second sack of popcorn and scattering it on the floor like a long-snouted hog. The popcorn lady lay still near the first popcorn sack, and the manager was backing up, shining his flashlight on Albert. The manager was shaking and staring over the top of his glasses. Just like Mr. Longnecker, he saw, but his eyes didn't believe what he saw.

Pat and I carried Albert out to the car and put him in the trunk. Then we went back in to see the rest of *Tarzan*.

When we went back into the theater, the manager, Mr. Roberts, gave Pat an over-the-glasses look that said he would sure like to search him. But you could tell he was too afraid to do that. He acted like he was afraid Pat might have a rattlesnake or a boa constrictor this time.

When Pat took his seat, all he said was, "Albert didn't even get to see the alligator."

Chapter 12

The Newspaper Route

Lynn Courtney was redheaded and freckle-faced, and he always wore a cap with the bill turned slightly to the side. This was because he was kinda cross-eyed. The bill of his cap being off to the side looked just right on Lynn, because one of his eyes was kinda off to the side.

That crossed left eye gave Lynn a lot of advantages over other people. He was an especially good baseball pitcher. You never could tell where he was throwing 'cause you couldn't tell where he was looking.

Lynn was not only cross-eyed and left-handed, he also had a newspaper route. He was the straightest newspaper-thrower you ever saw. He'd ride by a house before daylight on his bicycle, reach into the basket on the front of his bicycle, and pick out a newspaper that was folded just right. Then he'd reach back with his left arm and throw that newspaper. It would hit and bounce and skid and come to rest on the front porch right in front of the door.

Lynn stopped me in front of the ice cream parlor and asked me if I wanted to run his newspaper route while he and his mama and daddy took their vacation to Washington, D.C.

"Naw, Lynn, I wish I could, but I don't have a bicycle."

"Oh well, you can use my bicycle, an' I'll pay you four dollars a week."

"How many newspaper customers you got, anyway?" I frowned as I tried to figure.

"Fifty-nine on weekdays and seventy-four on Sundays."

Pat came walking up as I rubbed my chin and considered Lynn Courtney's proposition.

"What time do you deliver these newspapers?" I asked.

"Papers mostly get here about 5:30 in the morning. It takes about an hour, maybe an hour and fifteen minutes, to fold the papers an' get 'em delivered. Might take you an hour an' a half since you don't know the route too well."

I frowned and stomped my foot. "Aw shucks, that's right at milkin' time. My dad would never let me off for two weeks."

"What you askin' about?" Pat asked.

I turned to Pat. "Lynn wants me to take his newspaper route while he's gone on vacation."

"Let me run it for you." Pat walked over to Lynn Courtney, grabbed the bill of his cap, and straightened it over his forehead.

Lynn watched Pat until he got the bill of the cap centrally located over his forehead and stepped back. Then Lynn reached up and pulled the cap back to where it shaded the side of his head instead of his forehead.

"You ain't big enough." Lynn raised his eyebrows and looked down at Pat.

Pat stepped forward until the tip of his nose was about six inches from Lynn's long neck. "I can do anything you can do, an' most things I can do better."

"You can't run a newspaper route." Lynn waved Pat away with his hand.

"I can, too."

"You can't throw a newspaper from the road to the house. You can't carry fifty-nine papers on a weekday, an' I *know* you can't throw seventy-four heavy Sunday papers on a bicycle."

"If you can do it, I can do it."

"You don't even know how to handle a barkin', bitin' dog. Shelby Best's bulldog would pull you off of the bicycle 'fore you got around the corner."

"You mean dogs bite at you while you're delivering newspapers?"

Lynn Courtney swelled up and folded his arms across his chest. He raised his eyebrows and looked at Pat, or else somewhere close to Pat.

"I'd hit him with a newspaper," Pat suggested.

"Yeah, and then you'd have to get off and get the newspaper, an' he'd tear the britches off of you."

Pat shrugged his shoulders. "I'd give him the newspaper."

"That's why you couldn't run my newspaper route; you'd ruin it. You can't give newspapers to dogs. You gotta give 'em to my customers." Lynn turned and put his hand on my shoulder and looked sorta in my direction. "I'll let you run my paper route an' pay you four dollars a week. You could make eight dollars while I'm gone."

"Eight dollars!" Pat gasped.

Lynn nodded his head, still talking in my direction. "Yeah, and you can ride my bicycle. Just keep the tires inflated and don't leave it out in the rain."

"Ride your bicycle?" Pat's eyes brightened. "That brand new bicycle with the basket on the front and them carriers on the back?"

Lynn nodded his head. Then he raised his eyebrows and said to me, "Well, what'cha say? Ya wanna handle my newspaper route while I'm gone?"

I shook my head. "Daddy don't pay me for milkin' cows, but I gotta milk them cows. An' milkin' starts about the same time you get your newspapers. An' by the time the milkin's done, it's too late to deliver newspapers."

"Oh?" Lynn looked at me, and then he studied Pat. "I gotta get somebody dependable. We're gonna be leavin' day after tomorrow."

"I'll handle your newspaper route. I need to make some money. We're gonna be takin' our vacation in about three weeks. I'll handle your newspaper route." Pat pushed on Lynn for emphasis and attention.

"Will you deliver the newspapers even if the dogs bite you?"

Pat rolled his eyes and thought for a minute. "How many biting dogs are there?"

"Oh, there's a couple a dozen dogs, but there's only three real mean 'uns. They'll tear your britches plum off of you." Lynn Courtney was now looking sorta in Pat's direction.

Pat tugged on Lynn's leather jacket and looked up at him. "What d'ya do when they try to bite ya?"

"You have to ride by real fast and throw your paper 'fore they know you're comin'."

"Oh . . . Well, yeah, I'll do it."

Pat went into Armbruster's Store and charged a piece of chalk to Daddy. He ran along beside Lynn Courtney's bicycle, marking a chalk line on the curb in front of every house that was due to receive a newspaper.

The evening before Lynn was to leave on his vacation, Pat walked over to his house and rode his bicycle home. He let us all ride it, even Tina.

The next morning Mama woke Pat up at 5:30. He was still asleep when he rode off on the bicycle to Hurst's Drugstore, where the morning newspapers were left when the Continental Bus came through town.

Pat never got home 'til 9:30. His corduroy britches were torn on both legs and his face was red where he had cried.

"What took you so long? Did'ja have any trouble?" I asked.

Pat raised one leg sorely and slowly over the bicycle seat as he dismounted. He hobbled to the front porch and sat down on the swing. He shut his eyes and bit down on his lip. "That darned Lynn Courtney said they wasn't but three bitin' dogs on that route."

"Well, how many bitin' dogs were they?" I asked.

"Not more'n three hunnerd."

"Aw, they ain't three hunnerd dogs in this whole town."

"Try ridin' a bicycle down ever' street." Pat spoke glumly as he rubbed the bruises on his legs where his britches had been torn. He looked up at me and shook his head. "You can't ride a bicycle and throw a newspaper while a dog's got ahold of your britches leg." He shook his head and looked down at the floor of the front porch. "Them dogs saw me comin'."

"You didn't ride by fast enough," I suggested.

"Did'ja ever try ridin' a bicycle with fifty-nine heavy newspapers weightin' it down?"

"Well, what'cha gonna do? Give it up?" I asked.

"Give it up!" Pat shouted and frowned at me. He quit rubbing his bruised legs and climbed out of the porch swing. He stood as tall as he could and grinned as he spoke. "Me an' Albert are gonna deliver them newspapers tomorrow mornin'."

"Albert!"

"Yeah." Pat smiled at the thought. "I think I'll put Albert on top of that rear basket so he can climb up on his hind legs and lean over the side of that bicycle. First time he bites the ears off that white bulldog of Shelby Best's, I'll bet that dog'll quit chasin' newspaper boys on bicycles."

"Mebbe you better forget that newspaper route. Them dogs done see you ain't big enough to fight back."

Pat nodded. "I ain't very big," he rubbed his scratched leg, "but the next time I ride that route, I'm gonna have Albert Geronimo riding behind me. I'll strap him on that bicycle behind me. Some of them biting dogs, they're gonna get bit back."

"Oh no!" I stepped back. "He's liable to bite a dog's ear plum off!"

Pat grinned. "They's one dog I hope he does bite. He tried to pull me off the bicycle. I want to see him the next time he grabs my leg and ends up looking into Albert Geronimo's hungry mouth."

The next morning, I got Daddy to milk for me and I ran along behind Pat. I wanted to see what happened when Shelby Best's big white Shelby Best's big white bulldog met Albert.

I carried some rocks to throw at dogs, to keep them from running after Pat's bicycle. But I got left behind. I could see I wasn't needed.

Pat had tied Albert in his Boy Scout pack to the rear carrier of his bicycle, where the alligator could turn his long tooth snout to either side of the bicycle.

The bicycle was only three blocks from the drug store when a German Shepherd came running and barking at Pat. His head was within two feet of Pat's right leg. Then Albert raised his long ugly head and nipped the dog's long nose.

The dog yipped, jumped straight up, and clawed the air. He curled his tail between his legs and ran low and cowardly toward his house and hid under the front porch.

I cut across two streets so I could be at Shelby Best's house when Pat came riding by throwing newspapers.

Pat saw me and waved a folded newspaper at me, then threw it into the yard. "Albert Geronimo's done snapped at two dogs. I think he's cured 'em of chasin' this bicycle," he shouted.

Then he pulled another newspaper. It was for Shelby Best's house. Sure enough, their big white bulldog was lying on his belly on the grass, waiting for Pat to ride by.

He waited until Pat threw the newspaper, then he attacked.

He raced across the grass, the sidewalk, and was in the street, barking and coming up on Pat with his teeth glistening in the morning light.

Pat took a newspaper and tried to swat the huge bulldog. It swerved away, making Pat miss, then he raced in, bared his teeth, and was about to bite Pat's right britches leg.

Then Albert's long, toothy snout rose from his packsack perch on the rear of the bicycle. He opened his mouth wide and snapped at the bulldog's head just as it was about to bite Pat's leg.

Albert bit a glove-sized triangle out of that white dog's ear. Then he snapped for another bite, a better one.

The dog howled, his eyes got big and white with disbelief, and he came rolling head over heels down the street, trying with every roll to get farther and farther away from that bicycle with a built-in alligator. He limped to his feet and hobbled home with a big hole bit in his left ear.

Albert rose high in his perch, grinning as he chomped on his trophy.

After that ride, Pat had no more trouble with dogs. They took one look at him coming down the street, then yipped and ran under the house.

Chapter 13

Albert is Accused

"You lost any chickens, Mr. Templeton?" Police Chief McGruder asked when he quit blowing on his coffee after he came into our house on Friday evening.

"Well, yeah, I 'spect I have, one or two, maybe more." Daddy spoke kind of hesitatingly.

"Ever'body around here's lost a lot of chickens." Chief McGruder was looking at his coffee cup.

"They have?" Daddy asked.

"Yep."

"Got any tracks of skunks or coons or bobcats?" Daddy asked.

Chief McGruder shook his head. "No skunk, coon, possum, or bobcat tracks." Chief McGruder pressed his lips together, took a sip of coffee, and then looked at Daddy. "Just alligator tracks."

"Alligator tracks!" Me and Dad and Pat spoke the words at the same time.

"The tracks of your son's alligator are all over the neighborhood. He's quite a traveller. And he seems to have developed a taste for chickens. He gets 'em in broad

56

daylight. Herbert Davenport up the road from you has lost four or five. Seth Goforth down the road lost half a dozen. Bill Brashears across the creek from you, he don't know how many he's lost, but that alligator's been there. Bill says he sees white feathers from his leghorn chickens and alligator droppings on his place."

Daddy was looking down with a frown. Then he looked at Pat and kept his eyes on him until Pat looked up.

"You're gonna have to keep Albert up," he told Pat.

"He won't eat if I keep him penned up," Pat spoke.

"That don't make no never mind. We can't have an alligator running around here eatin' chickens. Next thing you know, he'll be eatin' dogs, an' then he'll be eatin' people."

Pat shook his head. A big tear formed in one eye and rolled slowly down his cheek as he shook his head. "Albert don't eat chickens."

"Oh yes he does." Chief McGruder cracked his fingers nervously. "Bill Brashears says he found white feathers and alligator droppings."

"He ain't never seen no alligator droppings. He couldn't tell alligator droppings from goat droppings." Pat almost smiled through the tears running down his cheek.

"Sounds bad, Pat," Daddy said. "We have lost some chickens."

"But Daddy," Pat's eyes were pleading, "that don't mean Albert got 'em!"

"He's an alligator, ain't he?" Chief McGruder rose to his feet and set his coffee cup on the table. "They ain't nothin' an alligator won't eat." He looked at Pat, and then at Daddy. "You know how we treat chicken-eatin' dogs. The quicker you shoot 'em, the better off ever'body is. If you wait 'til you catch 'em eatin' chickens, first thing you know, you ain't got no chickens."

"Thank you, Chief." Daddy got up from the table and shook hands with Chief McGruder.

They walked out of the kitchen and into the living

room. As they walked out the front door onto the porch, I followed them.

Chief McGruder turned to my dad. "I'll be glad to shoot that alligator for you."

"Thanks." I heard Daddy slap the chief of police on the shoulder. "It might be best to shoot him and get it over with. Any other road we followed would just string out the pain."

Pat looked at me, pleading for help with his eyes. I looked at the floor of the porch.

"That alligator hasn't caused anything but trouble." Daddy was looking at Pat. "He tore up the school and the grocery store, an' he caused a lot of screamin' at the picture show. He has been nothin' but trouble and expense."

"You want me to shoot him?" Chief McGruder asked.

Pat broke through the front door, sending the screen door flying. He ran up to Chief McGruder with his arms folded across his chest and tears streaming down his cheeks. "Albert's mine. Ain't nobody gonna kill Albert." Pat was looking the chief right in the face.

Chief McGruder reached down and unbuckled his holster and pulled out his pistol. He looked at Pat as he pulled the hammer back on the gun. Then he turned to Daddy. "Where's that alligator?"

Chief McGruder stepped off the front porch and started around the side of the house.

Pat raced around and stood in front of the chief. He placed his hands on his hips. "If you shoot Albert, you'll have to shoot me, too."

The chief stepped around Pat and pushed him to his side as he walked on around to the back of the house.

Pat stood there blinking for an instant. Then he ran to Daddy and dropped down on his knees. He put his arms around Daddy's legs and said, "Don't let him shoot Albert." Pat blinked a couple of times, and then he went on. "He's mine. If he has to be shot . . ." Pat shut his eyes. He pointed toward the chief of police. "I don't want him to shoot him."

Daddy nodded and patted his son on the shoulder. He licked his lips and clenched his jaw, and then he raised his hand. "Hold on a minute." He walked around the side of the house just as Chief McGruder raised his pistol, taking aim at something on the bottom step of the back porch. "The boy says he don't want you shootin' Albert," Daddy said.

"Huh?" Chief McGruder had already shut one eye and was taking aim. He looked at my dad with disbelief and disappointment.

"You gonna let this chicken-eater go?" the chief asked.

"My son says he will take care of him." Daddy turned around and put his hands on Pat's shoulders, who was now crying. "And he will take care of him."

Most of the time I hated the job of milking — sitting next to balky cows with cockleburs in their tails, switching your ears instead of flies — but when I had a problem, then milking was no trouble 'cause then I had time to sit and think.

That's what I did Saturday night after Chief McGruder said Pat was going to have to shoot Albert.

I couldn't forget Pat's tears. Made me nearly cry. Anything that hurts Pat, it hurts me.

I grinned when I thought about the way Pat folded his arms across his chest an' looked Chief McGruder in the face. Tears quit streamin' down Pat's face when he stood between the chief and Albert. Pat looked like a man standin' in front of a firin' squad, ready to be shot.

"If you shoot Albert, you'll have to shoot me, too." That's what Pat said, and he looked like he meant it. He said he knew Albert wasn't eating chickens.

I stopped milking and looked up, remembering how Pat had looked.

Pat said he was going to find proof that Albert wasn't eating our chickens and our neighbors' chickens.

Pat's chin was firm and determined. He was a finder. If he said he was going to find proof, well, if Pat said he was going to find anything, he'd find it.

Then I had another thought. What if Pat found proof that Albert *was* eating chickens? What would he do? Would he tell Daddy? I nodded. He would tell. He would tell the truth. Even to Tina.

Would he kill Albert? I shook my head. I knew how much Pat loved Albert. He would tell the truth, but he couldn't kill his friend.

I was anxious to find out what Pat had discovered.

Pat walked out to the barn the next morning before daylight. His lip was firm and determined, as usual. "I'm gonna find whatever it is that's eatin' these chickens."

"Bill Brashears says he found white leghorn feathers and —"

"And not Albert's droppin's." Pat's eyes challenged me. "I'm gonna find out what's eatin' these chickens." Then Pat looked at me. "Even if it is Albert."

Pat had his hand behind his hips and he was walking back and forth. He went to the door of the barn and looked outside. It was still dark.

"Mama says you're a finder. She says you can find anything. I bet you'll find out what's eatin' them chickens."

"I'm gonna find out, an' when I do," Pat raised his foot and stomped it on the barn floor, "I'm gonna make him wish he'd never accused Albert of bein' a chicken-eater."

"What'cha gonna do if you don't find out?" I asked.

Pat stared at me, not liking what I had said. He reached up and pounded the palm of his hand on the wall of the barn. "I've already put Albert back in his pen." He turned around and looked at me and stopped pounding the wall. "It ain't big enough for him no more."

"You mean if you find out he's the one, you'll —"

"I don't know what I'll do." Pat stomped out of the barn. When he got to the door, he turned and looked at me. "Albert don't like that chicken-wire pen. He's tasted freedom, an' he don't like to go back in there. He struggles and wrestles and looks real hurt when I put him in that little muddy pen."

"It's keep him in there or have him shot," I reminded Pat.

"Yeah, an' if he stays in that pen, he won't eat. He'll die."

Chapter 14

More Evidence

Shelby Best's cotton-colored hair looked like it came off of his white bulldog when he and his father climbed out of their station wagon in front of our house.

Albert Best was the president of the First National Bank, and he came walking toward our front door like he was in a hurry. Shelby waited at the station wagon, holding his dog with the bloody stubble of a left ear. Shelby looked at Pat like a happy smart alec that knows what's fixing to happen.

"Son, is your father home?" Mr. Best asked Pat.

Pat looked down at the ground. He slid off of the porch swing slowly and shook his head. He looked at me for help. But I couldn't help him.

"Daddy's down at the barn feedin' the cows."

Mr. Best took off his straw hat and began fanning his face. "Do you have an alligator here?"

Pat nodded his head glumly.

"My son says that you have an alligator that bit off White Night's left ear."

Pat rolled his eyes. "Yeah, he bit it off and ate it."

"He ate it!" Mr. Best stepped backward and looked around. "Do you mean you have an alligator that bit off my dog's ear and ate it?"

Pat nodded.

Mr. Best stared at Pat and then at me with utter disapproval. The corners of his mouth were turned down.

"Are you gonna have that alligator shot?" Mr. Best asked.

Pat shook his head.

"He might have rabies! He might have hydrophobia!"

Pat looked at me and I looked at him.

"That alligator'll have to be shot and his head sent off to the state capital."

Pat's eyes grew big and blinked. He clenched his lips together.

"I've already called Chief McGruder. He'll be here in a minute, an' when he gets here, he'll take care of that stinkin' alligator."

Pat was fighting back tears. "Albert ain't no stinkin' alligator."

"We may all have rabies." Mr. Best raised his hand and knocked on the door. "White Night has been vaccinated, but we haven't." Mr. Best shook his head.

"Will I have to take a shot?" Pat asked as he brought his hand up and felt of his left arm.

"If it's not too late." Mr. Best bobbed his head accusingly.

When nobody answered his knock on the door, Mr. Best turned to Pat. "Where's your mother? Where's your father? Where's your alligator?"

Pat and I looked down the road and saw Chief McGruder's police car approaching, leaving a trail of dust behind.

Pat turned from the approaching police car and put his hands over his head. He placed his head against the doorfacing.

Chief McGruder climbed out of his car. Before he

closed the door, he reached in the car and picked up a rifle. He cradled it in his arm as he approached the front porch. He stalked toward Pat and said, "I told you a month ago you shoulda had that alligator shot."

Pat turned from the doorfacing and stared at Chief McGruder. "Albert didn't do nothin' but protect me from that bulldog."

"Well, he's gotta be shot." Chief McGruder pulled back the lever on his rifle and put in a shell. "Where is he?"

Pat shook his head. "I ain't gonna tell ya."

"You're protectin' a rabid animal?"

"He ain't got rabies unless he got it from that square-jawed bulldog," Pat argued.

"Is he in that swamp?" Chief McGruder's eyes were narrow and cold.

"I ain't gonna tell ya."

Mr. Best and Chief McGruder turned to me.

"Where is that alligator?" McGruder asked.

I looked at Pat. His eyes begged me not to tell.

I lied. "Pat's the only one that knows where Albert is."

Mr. Best walked off of the porch and headed south toward the barn. "Where's Henry? I want to see your father."

Pat took off running. He got ahead of Mr. Best and Chief McGruder and shouted, "Daddy! Daddy! They've come to shoot Albert!"

Mama was the first one to come out of the barn. She reached out and clasped Pat to her chest as he dove into her arms. "What's the matter, Son?" Mama patted him on the back.

Pat turned and looked at Mr. Best and Chief Mc-Gruder. "They've come to shoot Albert." Pat began to cry.

Mama clung to Pat and looked over his shaking head. "What's he done now?"

Mr. Best was fanning his face with his fancy hat. "He bit half of White Night's ear off and ate it."

"He what?" Mama looked down at Pat and then at Mr. Best. "Who is White Night?"

"He's my dog." Mr. Best pointed his head back toward Shelby Best and the dog standing beside the station wagon.

Mama raised her head. "My son told me about your dog biting him and tearing his britches." She looked up at Mr. Best with a proud smile on her face. "He told me that after one trip with Albert on the bicycle behind him, he had no more trouble with dogs. Not with your dog or with any other dog."

"Yes, but what about rabies?" Mr. Best argued.

Daddy came out of the barn carrying two filled milk buckets, one in each hand. "What's goin' on out here?" he asked.

"Your son's alligator bit my dog." Mr. Best stalked toward Daddy.

Daddy set the milk buckets down slowly. He raised his head and looked the banker square in the face. "Your dog bit my son."

"But that alligator, it may have rabies," Mr. Best insisted.

Daddy stared at the ground in front of him for a minute with a smile. Then he looked up at Mr. Best. "Alligators are cold-blooded animals; they are not carriers of rabies."

"What!" Mr. Best and Chief McGruder spoke at the same time.

Daddy shook his head. "Albert might bite dogs that attack my son, but he can't give 'em rabies."

Chief McGruder looked at his rifle with disappointed eyes.

Daddy picked up the two milk buckets and started walking toward the house. He raised the lid on the ten-gallon milk can on the back porch and poured both buckets of milk into the can. Then he replaced the lid on the milk can.

"An alligator can't give any animal rabies, not even a dog," he repeated.

Chief McGruder and Mr. Best glanced at each other

significantly, like two men who were suddenly out of place.

Daddy turned his two milk buckets upside down and set them on top of the milk can. Then he turned to Mr. Best and Chief McGruder. "You're both guests on my place. I'm sorry your dog attacked my son and got bit by my son's alligator." He looked at Pat, and then turned back to the two men. "I'll thank you to get off of my property." He pointed his hand toward their cars.

"Well now . . ." Mr. Best swelled. "Henry, I've loaned you a lot of money, and you still owe most of it."

Daddy cut in. "Yeah, an' we're puttin' it to good use. We're taking our vacation in a few days. By the time we return, Pat and I will have figured out what to do with his pet. Please leave it to us."

Chief McGruder and Mr. Best stood out in the street talking to each other for a few moments. Then Mr. Best and Shelby got in the station wagon and drove away. In a little bit, Chief McGruder drove away, too.

Albert slept through it all. He was still on the bottom step of the back porch.

Chapter 15

Pat Learns the Truth

When Pat came in the barn, he looked at me and then looked away. He stood with his back turned to me, avoiding my eyes.

"Well, did you find out what's been eatin' our chickens and our neighbors' chickens?" I asked.

Pat looked at me out of the side of his eye, like I had said something that hurt. Finally, he nodded his head. It was a sad, slow, unhappy nod. He clenched his jaws and tightened his lips like he was going to swallow something big and heavy and unpleasant.

"Well, was it Albert?" I asked.

Pat turned to me, looked me straight in the face, and nodded. A tear formed in one eye, and it rolled slowly down his cheek. His lower lip quivered, and for a moment he couldn't speak. He wiped the tear away with his hand, and then he spoke.

"I followed Albert. I found out he's an alligator. I found out he eats chickens."

Pat stood there with his face wrinkled, blinking back huge, wet tears.

I put my milk bucket down and went to Pat and put my arms around him. I patted him on the back and hugged him. He really cried when I hugged him.

After a little bit, he stepped back and held me at arm's length. He looked me in the eye. "What would you do if they were gonna shoot me 'cause I ate chickens?"

"What?"

"Yeah." Pat sighed and blinked his tear-reddened eyes. "Wouldn't you fight to keep 'em from shootin' me?"

"Yeah, I sure would."

"Well, that's what I'm gonna do. I'm gonna fight to keep Albert."

"Did you find out for sure that he's a chicken-eater?" I asked.

Pat nodded. "Yeah, I followed him, an' he's smart. He's smart in the head." Pat pointed to his head. "He looks back as often as he looks in front of him. He took off for the Bill Brashears place, an' he went there straight as an arrow. He knew where he was goin'." Pat shook his head, and then he looked at me. "An' he knew what he was gonna do when he got there."

"Did you see him catch a chicken?" I asked.

"Yeah, but it warn't easy. He looked back so often that I had to stay way behind. At times he ran. He's got a trail, but it's an alligator trail. It wasn't easy to follow. He got there 'fore I did, an' I liked to never saw him." Pat pounded his open hand against his forehead. "Albert looked just like a dead piece of wood. He crawled up real close to where some chickens were. He just stayed real still until a chicken came close, and then he jumped and snapped. That chicken never cackled twice."

"Did you see him eat it?" I asked.

"Yeah, I seen him eat it."

"You gonna tell Daddy?"

Pat looked at me and bit his lip. "I don't know."

"You gonna tell Chief McGruder?"

"I ain't gonna tell Chief McGruder nothin'."

"He'll shoot Albert if you tell him."

"Yeah, I know."

"But you gotta tell. You gotta tell somebody."

"Well," Pat looked at me, "I told you."

"You know if he's a chicken-eater, in a little while, he'll be a cat-eater. And then in a little while he'll be a dog-eater. Then one mornin' you'll wake up an' find he's a people-eater."

"Yeah, I know. I done found out Albert's an alligator."

"Well, what'cha gonna do?"

"I don't think it's any fairer to shoot Albert 'cause he's an alligator than it is to shoot me 'cause I like to fish."

"Yeah, but catchin' fish is legal. Catchin' chickens ain't."

We went to church the next Sunday morning. This time Pat didn't fuss or complain or anything. He was ready to go. I noticed he really listened and watched Brother Edmondston when he gave his sermon. When Brother Edmondston called for prayer, I could see Pat's lips working as he prayed. Even Mama and Tina noticed how prayerful Pat suddenly was.

I knew Pat was praying for the Lord to tell him how to save his friend and playmate, Albert Geronimo.

If prayers will save anything, Pat's prayer would save Albert, 'cause he was still prayin' when the preacher got through.

Pat looked at me with a bright look in his eyes. He looked like he already knew what he was gonna do.

Tina shrugged her shoulders and looked at me. "What can prayers do for a chicken-eatin' alligator?"

Chapter 16

A Change in Plans

"Mama, why do we always have to go to California on our vacation?" Pat asked.

"Well, Son, there's the Pacific Ocean and Yosemite Valley, and, of course, there's Hollywood. We nearly always see a movie star if we stop there and wait long enough."

"Aw, who wants to see a movie star?"

"Well I do." Tina sauntered up, prissing her hips, acting like she was Ginger Rogers.

"I wanna see Gary Cooper." I licked my lips, firmed my jaws, and squinted my eyes, trying to look like Gary Cooper.

Pat gave me a look that said I wasn't helping him very much. Then he spoke. "I'd just ruther go to Florida."

"Do you think the Atlantic Ocean would be more fun than the Pacific?" Mama asked as she sprinkled water on the starched shirts at the ironing board.

Pat quit looking at me and turned to Mama. "I'd just ruther go to Florida." He got to his feet and looked at me. "I done seen California."

70

"But why Florida?" Tina frowned. "They's no movie stars in Florida. They ain't nothin' there but oranges and grapefruit and Miami Beach." Tina curled her lips and squinched her nose with disapproval.

"Why do you want to go to Florida, Son?" Mama raised a shirt up and flicked the droplets of water off of the shirt, getting it ready to iron.

"Wouldn't we have to go through Georgia to get to Florida from here?" Pat asked.

Suddenly, all eyes turned to Pat. Even Daddy looked at Pat for a minute. He rustled his newspaper, then looked at the paper as if he were reading, but he spoke. "Oh, I suppose we could detour Georgia if we wanted to."

"Oh, I don't wanna detour Georgia," Pat said quickly.

Daddy and everybody else studied Pat silently. What was he up to?

"Why do you want to go through Georgia?" Tina frowned.

"Yeah," I laughed, "what's Georgia got that California ain't got?"

I watched an innocent smile lighten Pat's face before he spoke. "Okefenokee Swamp."

Mama, Daddy, Tina, and I all stopped what we were doing and spoke at the same time. "What?"

"What did you say, Son?" Daddy rose from his big rocker. He folded his newspaper and put it under his arm. Then he took his glasses off his nose and put them in his coat pocket. He approached Pat. "What's this about a swamp?"

Pat looked at Daddy with innocent, pleading eyes. "I asked my teacher, Mrs. Phillips, where there was a swamp, and she said there was a swamp in Georgia and another one in Florida."

"But why would you wanna go see a swamp?" Daddy was swinging his arm, gesturing with his folded newspaper, when all of a sudden he stopped. He blinked a couple of times while the sudden realization soaked in. Then he looked at the floor as he guessed. "Albert Geronimo!"

Tina stepped forward. "You want us to take a vacation just so you can drop off your ole alligator in some ole nasty *swamp?*"

Pat smiled and nodded his head.

"Oh no." Daddy slapped his folded newspaper against his britches leg. "We're not going to Florida."

Mama stood holding a dampened shirt in front of her looking it over. Then she laid the shirt on the ironing board. She didn't look at Pat, but she spoke. "You wanna go by a swamp on the way to Florida so you can release your alligator where he'll have a chance to be an alligator." Mama looked up at Pat as she continued. "Isn't that right?"

Pat nodded his head.

"Well, I'll be." Daddy stood there with his newspaper held at arm's length. He never could read a newspaper without his glasses on. He was looking over the newspaper, staring at Pat. He knew Pat was gonna talk Mama into taking a vacation to Florida, and the rest of us would just have to go along.

Chapter 17

Poolside Problems

When we got ready to start our vacation, Pat located a battered old violin box to carry Albert in.

None of us really wanted to take Albert, especially Tina. She didn't like bein' in the same town with Albert, let alone bein' in the same car.

We left Pricilla with Mrs. Baggett, because she liked cats and would take good care of her until we got home. We knew Big Mack would just go over to the Davenports and scratch on their back door when he got hungry. Rusty Davenport and his father agreed to milk the cows and tend to the chickens and hogs 'til we got back.

Albert refused to ride inside his box. He slammed and slapped it and growled and hissed until Pat took the top off of the box and Albert climbed out and got in his lap. Then Albert grinned that long-snouted toothy grin of his to say he was happy and satisfied.

Pat rode on the left side of the back seat and I rode in the middle. Tina rode almost outside the rear right door. She stayed as far away from me and Pat and Albert as she could get and still hang on to the car.

We really had trouble when we tried to find a place to stay. At one motel, Albert, being an alligator, could smell the swimming pool half a mile off. He started climbing out of the car and heading for the swimming pool for a refreshing dip before we all got out of the car. The motel manager took one look at Pat and Albert and began shaking his head and waving his hands.

We had to put Albert in his box, tie it up, and put it in the trunk of the car and hide it before we could find a motel that would take us.

Little Rock, Arkansas, had three nervous motel owners who refused to let us have a room. But there was one motel owner that just didn't know he had Albert as a guest.

Pat didn't take Albert to the swimming pool until after ever'body gave up swimming and left. Then Pat put on his swimming suit and carried Albert in his violin box to the edge of the swimming pool. Pat looked around to the right and to the left guiltily. Then he opened the box and let Albert crawl out and dive into the swimming pool. Albert was so hot and dry that he swam under the water halfway across the pool.

I was standing there beside the swimming pool holding the violin box, and Pat had his feet in the shallow part of the pool.

Albert had gone to the bottom of the swimming pool looking for some mud when Pat and I heard some doors open. We heard giggles and laughs and the tinkle of ice in glasses. Two young couples in bathing suits came running from their motel rooms toward the enclosed swimming pool.

Pat looked at me and I looked at him when the couples got to the swimming pool. Fortunately, they didn't get in the water. They set their drinks on a table beside the pool and started chatting.

I opened the empty violin box and looked at it. Then I looked at Pat, and then at the swimming pool. There was Albert as plain as an alligator can be, resting on the bottom near the drain.

Pat and I looked at Albert and then looked at each other. We wondered how long he was going to stay under the water. Then I wondered what was going to happen when he came to the top.

The couples were laughing and tinkling glasses. Pat got up and walked over to the edge of the swimming pool and looked down toward the bottom. He was worried about Albert. He was wondering how long he could stay under the water, wondering if he had drowned. I was kinda glad Albert was on the bottom of the pool. But some way we had to get him out and get him in that violin box and back into the trunk of the car.

"They're drinkin' whiskey," Pat whispered.

"Yeah. We'd better go."

Pat shrugged his shoulders. "If Mama sees them drinkin' whiskey, she'll twist our ears." Pat looked toward our motel room. Then he turned and looked at the couples pouring whiskey. They were laughing and giggling.

"We'd better go," I argued.

Pat turned to me and shook his head. "I can't go." He pointed to the swimming pool. "Albert's still down there."

I walked over to the edge of the swimming pool and looked down into the clear, lighted water. There was Albert, still on the bottom. "Is he dead?" I asked.

Pat leaned over the pool and stared for a long time. Then he turned back to me and shook his head. "Naw, he's wiggling his tail a little bit."

"What're we gonna do?"

"Well, I can't go to the room. I'm not gonna leave 'til Albert comes up."

"You better not wait 'til he comes up." I pointed at the whiskey bottles.

Pat leaned back over the pool and spoke without looking at me. "I wonder how deep that water is?"

"I don't know, but it looks awful deep to me."

"Yeah, an' he's right on the bottom, right under the diving board, in the deepest part."

"Well, I ain't gonna go get him." I gave Pat a haughty shrug. "He ain't my alligator."

" 'Fraidy cat." Pat turned and dove into the water.

I ran along beside the pool, following Pat as he swam under water toward the drain at the bottom of the pool. Down Pat went, swimming with his arms and kicking with his feet. When Pat finally got to the bottom, Albert turned his head and swam away. Albert got to the surface before Pat did and began swimming along the edge of the pool closest to me. But there wasn't any place for him to climb out. Then he swam toward the shallow end of the pool toward the tables where the people were sitting.

Pat came to the surface of the pool. "Where is he? Did you see him?"

I just pointed my finger at Albert as he swam under the rope marking the shallow water and headed for even shallower water.

Pat took off as fast as he could.

But he wasn't fast enough. Albert got to the wading end of the pool. He raised his two front feet and put them on the wall drain. Then he raised his long snout over the edge of the pool.

The tall, blond-headed young man who was facing the pool lowered his head and stared around the whiskey bottle. He looked at the woman across the table from him and said, "I think I need a drink."

"You've had enough," she said as she pushed the whiskey bottle away.

The man rose to his feet, staring at Albert's head. He was watching Albert try to climb out of the pool when he spoke. "Do you see what I see?"

The heavy-set, dark-haired man was leaning back in his chair. When he looked over his shoulder and saw Albert, he turned his chair over and fell backward. He crawled off of the back of his chair and sat on his hands and knees, staring at Albert. He turned and looked back at his three companions and spoke as he raised one hand and pointed at Albert's long snout. "That looks like an alligator."

The tall, blond man walked around from behind the table. He was looking at Albert, too. "I told you we shouldn't'a bought that cheap whiskey."

Pat swam up behind Albert, reached up, and threw the alligator over his shoulder.

By then both couples were on their feet, watching Pat carry Albert across his shoulder as he walked across the pool and started climbing out.

Pat shifted Albert from his left shoulder to his right shoulder as he walked by the two couples.

"That sure looks like a real alligator." The heavy-set, dark-haired young man blinked his drunk sodden eyes and reached for the whiskey bottle on the table.

"Hey, boy," the other man said to Pat. "Where did you get a rubber float that looks that much like an alligator?"

Pat stopped and turned his head toward the couples. When he did, Albert turned his head, but it was in the other direction.

The dark-haired young man was pouring whiskey, but he wasn't hitting his glass. He was watching Albert.

Albert was struggling, clawing, and kicking, trying to get away.

Pat finally pulled Albert to his chest and turned and spoke to the tall, blond man. "He ain't no rubber float."

Right then Albert kicked his way free from Pat's grasp and started crawling back toward the cool swimming pool. Pat ran after him, but when he grabbed Albert by the tail, Albert turned around and opened his mouth fifteen inches wide and growled. Pat held on to his tail, but Albert crawled on to the edge of the swimming pool and dove in.

The couples stared at each other for a disbelieving instant. Finally, the woman next to the swimming pool gasped. "That *is* an alligator!" With her words, the table exploded. Both women jumped on top of the table. The two men held their drinks for an instant and then dropped them.

Pat dove into the swimming pool, swimming after Albert.

The two young men walked over to the swimming pool and stood beside me at the edge of the pool, watching Pat swimming under water trying to catch Albert.

But there was no catching Albert. He was headed for the drain at the bottom of the pool.

Pat came up for air at the rope. He gasped a couple of times and then turned to me. "Albert's goin' to the bottom again."

"I think he got too dry during the trip," I spoke.

The dark-haired man turned to me. "Is that a real alligator?"

I nodded my head.

The tall, blond man turned to me and pointed his finger at Pat. "What's he doin' in there with an alligator?"

"That's my brother Pat," I answered calmly.

"What's he doin' in there?" The blond man spoke as the two women walked up. One of the women put her hands on her knees and leaned over the edge of the pool. "That boy's trying to catch an alligator?" she asked.

"He's just tryin' to catch Albert. Albert's his best friend," I explained.

The man pointed his finger at Pat, who was swimming along the bottom of the pool trying to head off Albert at the drain.

"You mean that alligator's that boy's . . ." He turned to me and gulped and then looked back, his finger still pointing at Pat. "You mean that boy's tryin' to catch that alligator?"

I nodded.

"He ain't afraid of him?"

"Naw, he's a pet alligator. They go to the picture show together."

"The picture show!" The blonde woman turned and stared at me with amazement.

"They go ever'where together."

"Even in the swimming pool?" she asked.

I nodded. "Yeah, they swim together all the time."

The man looked at the heavy-set, dark-haired man. "Hey, that boy's havin' trouble catchin' his pet. Let's go help him."

The other man turned and stared at his companion. "Did you see those teeth?"

The tall, blond man already had his arms folded back and was ready to dive into the pool. "Come on; that boy needs some help." He dove into the pool and started swimming toward Pat and Albert.

"I'm gonna help, too." The blonde woman jumped into the pool, feet first.

The heavy-set young man reached his hand out toward his companion. "You drunk enough to swim with a pet alligator?"

The dark-haired girl looked at her friend for an instant. Then she grinned and blinked. "If that boy ain't afraid of that alligator, then I'm not, either." She jumped in.

In an instant, there were six people in the pool, including me, swimming and chasing Albert.

When Pat came up for air, the blonde woman went down, and when she came up for air, the dark-haired man went down.

Nobody could catch Albert. At one time, even the blonde woman had Albert by the tail. But when she grabbed his tail, he turned his head around and snapped his fifteen-inch snout at her fingers, making her scream and draw back her hand. Then Albert went on his merry way.

"I can catch him." Pat climbed out of the pool and sat on the edge of the concrete pool. He waved me and the others out of the pool. After we got out and stood over him at the edge of the pool, Pat began slapping his open palm against the concrete edge of the pool. "I'll catch him like I used to do back at the swamp. I used to call him to me, an' he always came." Pat pounded his open palm against the edge of the pool. He looked up at me. "Albert can feel the vibrations. Watch him turn his head and look at me."

Sure enough, Albert turned his head and stared at Pat.

"Come here, Albert." Pat slapped his palm against the concrete again.

Albert studied me and the two young men. Then he looked at the two women.

Pat waved his hands for them to step back, away from him.

When they did, Albert turned and swam to Pat. He climbed out on the bank with a nudge from Pat and curled up in Pat's lap — the happiest, most contented alligator you ever saw.

Pat and I put Albert in the violin box. As we walked toward our car to put Albert in a safe place, we heard the blond man say to his companions, "I don't think it *was* the bad whiskey."

Chapter 18

Parting in Georgia

We stopped at the Waycross Motel after we had almost crossed Georgia.

Mama said you could turn an alligator loose in Waycross, Georgia, and he could walk to the swamp.

Pat and I found out that weren't necessarily true. We talked to Mr. Stallings at the filling station across the street from the motel.

Mr. Stallings wiped his hands on an oilcloth. "You say you wanna go on the Okefenokee Swamp where there's alligators?"

Pat nodded his head.

"Well, they's not many alligators there any more." Mr. Stallings lit a cigarette while our car was being filled with gasoline. "Alligator-skinners killed off most of the alligators 'fore they passed a law making it illegal to kill an alligator." Mr. Stallings shook his head with disapproval. "They's hundreds of 'em out there if you get away from the roads and the boat trails."

"There are?" Pat's eyes lit up. "How do you find where there's alligators?"

"Like I said, you gotta go where there's no roads or boat trails."

"Why's that?" I asked.

"They ain't no fool stupid 'nuff to hunt an alligator on foot."

"Oh," Pat nodded thoughtfully, knowing he had to go where there were no boats or trails or roads 'fore he could find a safe place to release Albert Geronimo.

"If you was standin' right here an' you wanted to go where there was alligators, how'd you go?" Pat asked.

"Well, if I was goin' from here to where there's alligators, I'd head over toward Hopkins where the Suwanee River tries to drain the west side of the Okefenokee Swamp. Take the Calico Road out of Hopkins. You'll run outa road about Shantytown. Just to th' other side of Shantytown there's moss and guicksand that'll stop any man. If'n you'll sit real still and hide behind a water-logged cypress just at daylight or just before dark, you'll see alligators, some of 'em eight an' ten foot long."

"That's where I'm gonna go." Pat clapped his hands together.

Mr. Stallings put the cap on our gas tank. "A boy your size," he pointed at Pat, "ain't got no business lolly-gaggin' around no alligators. They'll have you for supper if you do."

Pat looked at me and smiled.

The next morning when Mama and Daddy and Tina and Pat and I climbed into the car, Pat leaned forward to talk to Mama. For some reason, when he wanted something done, he didn't ask Daddy; he asked Mama.

"Is there any way we can go through Hopkins on our way to Jacksonville?" Pat asked.

"Hopkins? Where on earth is Hopkins?" Mama turned and looked at Pat.

"It's right down that way." Pat pointed toward the southeast.

"Why on earth do you want to go to Hopkins?" Mama fanned herself with a road map.

" 'Cause that's where alligators are," Pat spoke quickly.

Daddy took his foot off the accelerator and turned toward Mama. "Is that where you want to release Albert Geronimo?" Daddy asked.

Pat nodded.

Mama put her hand on Daddy's arm. "Maybe it's on the road to Jacksonville," she suggested. She ran her finger down the map between Waycross, Georgia, and Jacksonville, Florida. Then she turned and looked at me and Pat. "Where on earth is Hopkins?"

"I don't know," Pat shrugged. "I just know it's southeast of Waycross."

Daddy put on the brakes and pulled over to the side of the road. He turned and looked at me and Pat sitting in the back seat. "Is that where we get rid of Albert Geronimo?"

Pat looked at me and we nodded our heads together.

"Well, I say let's go there." Tina nodded her head.

Daddy turned the car around and headed us back to Waycross. We stopped at Mr. Stallings' station again to get directions on how to get to Hopkins, and from Hopkins to Shantytown and the Suwanee River.

We had to go all the way back through Waycross and take the highway toward Valdosta, to Glenmore, Manor, and Argyle. Then we turned off on a dirt road and headed toward Hopkins.

We crossed a wooden bridge over the Suwanee River. Outside of town, the marsh grass on the side of the road was already window-high on our car. Daddy stopped and backed up all the way to Hopkins.

Mama and Daddy went into the Hopkins General Store while Pat and I carried Albert Geronimo in the violin case to the southeast through the tall, squishy marsh grass, trying to follow the east bank of the swamp-choked Suwanee River.

We finally came on a tall, gray-headed black man in a battered straw hat.

Pat shouldered the violin case and spoke to the man. "Is this Calico Road?"

"Yep, it sho' is. It's what's left of Calico Road."

"Are we on the road to Shantytown?"

The man took off his straw hat and shooed the mosquitos out of his face. " 'Tain't no road to Shantytown; 'tain't no Shantytown no mo'."

"No Shantytown?" Pat and I looked at each other and then back at the weathered face of the old man.

He shook his head. "Shantytown was a catfish town built on stilts. It done melted and gone away. Ever'body done moved to Chicago."

"Chicago!" Pat frowned and looked at the ground, and then he said, "We're lookin' for alligators."

"Alligators!" The old man's face creased into a solemn grin. He shook his head. "Alligators most all gone."

Pat shifted the violin case to his other shoulder. "Is there any place around here where an alligator could live?"

"Oh, they's alligator holes not more'n a hundred yards from here."

"Alligator holes?" Pat and I looked at each other.

"What's an alligator hole?" Pat asked.

"Oh, when it's hot an' dry like this," the man spread his left hand toward the sea of marsh grass, "them alligators dig holes and make wallowing places."

"Can you show us a wallowing hole?" Pat studied the tall, gray-headed man.

The man nodded his head and waved toward us. "Jest follow ole Amos."

Suddenly, Pat and I noticed Amos was wearing rubber boots as he plowed his arms through marsh grass that was even taller than his head.

I held on to Amos' britches leg, and Pat held on to my belt as we swished through the swampy marshland.

Amos turned and glanced behind him at me and Pat.

"We're in the swamp now." He stared at Pat's and my tennis shoes, already blackened with swamp mud. He turned and pointed his long, dark arm at a dead cypress tree. "They's a spring that trickles out of the ground 'neath that ole dead cypress. There's bound to be an alligator hole somewhere around that spring water."

We swished along through the mud until finally we reached the trunk of the dead cypress. The mud was now neary knee-deep, and the marsh grass was trampled down.

Our guide stopped and pointed his arm at the matted, trampled marsh grass. "They's an alligator hole 'neath there, but I don't reckon they's no alligator under thar. He'd a heard us comin', an' he's scattered by now."

Pat looked at me, and then he looked at his violin case and lowered it slowly to the ground.

"You got a violin? You gonna play some music for the alligators?" The old man laughed as Pat wiped the mud off of his violin box.

"Ain't got no violin," Pat growled. He put his hands on his hips, staring at Amos. "You can go now."

Amos looked at me and Pat. "Boy, you's in the Okefenokee Swamp."

Pat shook his head. "We can find our way out."

"You gonna wait here for an alligator?" Amos asked.

Pat shook his head. I knew he didn't want to open the violin box and release Albert while the man was watching. Pat sat down on top of the violin box and stared at Amos, waiting for him to leave.

Amos shook his head. "There's a town about two miles down river." He pointed to the south. Then he turned around and pointed to the north. "Hopkins is about half a mile that way." He looked at Pat again. "Boy, you sure you want Amos to leave?"

Pat nodded his head.

The old man nodded his head. "Well, when you start walkin' outa here, head to the northwest, and walk slow. Be sure to give them cotton-mouthed water moccasins and them diamond-back rattlers time to get out of your path."

Pat and I looked at each other with wide and worried eyes.

"Water moccasins and rattlers!" I jumped to my feet. "Mr. Amos, I think I'll go when you go."

Pat remained sitting on his violin case. He was looking at the ground. Finally, he looked up. "I ain't ready to go."

I nodded. Whatever Pat was gonna do, I was gonna do. I turned to the old man. "Thank you, Mr. Amos. Thank you very much. We'll find our way out."

Amos nodded his head and began walking away.

Pat and I waited until the squish of his booted feet disappeared. Then we opened the violin case slowly and quietly and leaned it over.

Albert raised his long, toothy snout and peeked over the sides of the box. He climbed out slowly, setting his two front feet in the muddy marsh grass. He pulled his hind legs and his long tail out of the box slowly, studying his new location.

Albert took three fast steps into the grass-covered marsh hole, and then stopped. He turned his head slowly and looked at Pat for an instant. Then he wiggled his tail and crawled into the marsh grass and disappeared in the alligator hole.

Pat and I rose to our feet slowly and stared at the trembling marsh grass. Then we looked at each other and shrugged our shoulders.

Pat tucked his hand in mine as we started walking back to the cypress tree. He stopped and took another look back to the southeast at Albert's alligator hole.

We whistled to keep each other company as we made our way back to Hopkins through the dense marsh grass.

Mama and Daddy were sitting in the car and Tina was astraddle the car hood when we got back to Hopkins with our empty violin box.

"Did'ja let him go?" Tina made a motion on top of the car hood as if she were riding a horse.

Pat nodded his head and opened the car door. He started to stick the violin box in. Then he stopped and looked at the box. He sighed as he lifted the box out and pressed it to his chest and hugged it for an instant. Then he carried it to the trash barrel on the south side of the General Store.

"Guess I won't be needin' that violin box no more." Pat dropped the empty box in the trash barrel. He looked at the box for a long time, then he turned toward the car.

Pat was fighting back tears. He held the car door open 'til Tina got in. She got in slowly, looking at Pat, watching him blink his eyes and tighten his lips as a tear streamed down his cheek.

As the car drove away from Hopkins, Pat turned around and looked back. He wiped away the tear.

"They's some things that when you love them, you have to give 'em up."

Mama turned around in the front seat and held her arm out to Pat. Daddy nodded and kept driving. Me and Tina, we just watched Pat.

He was crying. But he was happy.